EDITED BY MICHELE PAULE

THOUGHTLINES

A NEW WINDMILL ANTHOLOGY OF CHALLENGING TEXTS

CONSULTANTS:
DEBORAH EYRE and MICHAEL JONES

Heinemann
New Windmills

Heinemann Educational Publishers
Halley Court, Jordan Hill, Oxford OX2 8EJ
A division of Harcourt Education Limited

Heinemann is a registered trademark of
Harcourt Education Limited

OXFORD MELBOURNE AUCKLAND
JOHANNESBURG BLANTYRE GABORONE
IBADAN PORTSMOUTH NH (USA) CHICAGO

Selection, introductions and activities © Michele Paule, 2002

First published 2002
Second edition published 2002

06 05 04 03 02
10 9 8 7 6 5 4 3 2 1

British Library Cataloguing in Publication Data is available
from the British Library on request.

ISBN 0 435 13071 4

All the web links for this book can be accessed via
www.heinemann.co.uk/hotlinks and by typing in express code 0595P

Photographs: p69 Brian and Cherry Alexander/Hans Reinhard;
pp79, 101 Popperfoto; p124 Photofusion/Crispin Hughes
Cover Image: Stone/Jan Franz
Cover design by Forepoint
Typeset by ⊼ Tek-Art, Croydon, Surrey

Printed and bound in the United Kingdom by Clays Ltd, St Ives plc

Tel: 01865 888058 www.heinemann.co.uk

Contents

Introduction for Teachers

The extracts in this book have been chosen to challenge, stimulate and encourage further reading in able students at Key Stage 3. As with any other group of students, those who might fall under this definition will have a broad range of interests, skills and experience.

The anthology is arranged in sections to match the demands of the Framework for Teaching English Years 7–9:

- Looking at Language   (Sections 1 and 2)
- On Being a Reader   (Sections 3 and 4)
- From Reading to Writing   (Sections 5 and 6)
- Authors and their Craft   (Section 7).

Within these sections texts are grouped thematically, and each group of texts includes a range of genres, cultures and periods. The extracts themselves have been chosen from a range of sources that students might not necessarily meet in the course of their studies at Key Stage 3, but which can be linked to set texts/key themes. Your choice of texts within each section may also depend on the age and maturity of the group you are teaching – for example, you may find it more fitting to use the Antarctic and Captain Scott texts from 'On Being a Reader' in Year 7, and the extracts on gender and speech in 'You Just Don't Understand' and 'The Generation Gap' in Year 9.

At the end of each section you will find activities based on the texts – these have been tied into the Framework Objectives. The range of activities is designed to encourage close textual analysis, discussion and independent study/research/further reading. While it is possible for students to undertake the full range of activities independently, it is anticipated that the close study questions will be used interactively by teachers and adapted to suit the focus and needs of the class.

The 'Authors and Their Craft' section consists of reflections and advice on the writing process within a range of genres – these extracts suggest activities which encourage a high level of reflection.

Teachers may wish to use the extracts to focus on particular textual features or literary techniques to support their set text analysis or as extension/alternative material. An exemplar chart has been prepared on page x to suggest possible routes through the anthology using this approach.

Michele Paule

Introduction for Students

In this book you will find extracts from fiction, travel writing, journals, plays, screenplays, articles, poems, advertisements, advice to writers, parodies, history, web-based writing and transcripts of conversations.

You will find a whole range of types of writing grouped under thematic headings – this gives you the chance to look at how writers treat the same subject in different ways: for example, in 'The Generation Gap', you can compare the ways in which parent/child conflict is explored in *The Winter's Tale*, *Have the Men Had Enough?* and *Buffy the Vampire Slayer*.

Although the extracts are grouped under broad themes, the subject matter is not the main reason for their inclusion. The extracts offer a range of angles on a subject, or demonstrate particular styles and techniques. The activities at the end of each section help you to explore the ways in which you might respond as a reader, as well as giving a greater understanding of the writers' purposes, concerns and techniques.

The texts I have chosen the extracts from are readily available in bookshops, libraries or on the internet. I hope you feel inspired to read on…

Michele Paule

Table 1: Approaches to the Texts

Approach	Texts
Openings	*Pride and Prejudice*; *The Sheep Pig*; *The Princess Bride*; 'The Miller's Tale'; *Have The Men Had Enough?*
Language change	'The Miller's Tale'; *The Defense of Poesy*; *High Fidelity*; *Buffy the Vampire Slayer*
Narrative voice & viewpoint	'Deeper than Colour'; *A Telephone Call*; *Captain Scott's Diary*; 'Of Parents and Children'; *Have the Men Had Enough?*; *Jane Eyre*
Character & mood through dialogue	*Pride and Prejudice*; 'Bernice Bobs Her Hair'; *Jane Eyre*; *The Princess Bride*; *Screenwriting*
Creating expectations	*Jane Eyre*; *Pride and Prejudice*; 'Kit Bag'; 'The Miller's Tale'
Dramatic technique	*The Winter's Tale*; *Buffy the Vampire Slayer*; *Screenwriting*
Audience and purpose	The Lonely Planet; 'Guidance for Visitors'; Atlas Travel; 'Captain Scott's Tomb'; *Scott and Amundsen*; 'Things my Girlfriend...'; 'It's a Boy Thing'; *Tips for Journalists*
Creation of humour	'Things My Girlfriend...'; US Navy Transcript; 'Miss Mix'; 'Filboid Studge'; Communicating Feelings in Poems; *Buffy the Vampire Slayer*; 'The English Exam'
Settings – physical; social; cultural	*Captain Scott's Diary*; The Lonely Planet; 'Guidance for Visitors'; Atlas Travel; *The Princess Bride*; *Pride and Prejudice*; 'Deeper Than Colour'; *Jane Eyre*
Structure of texts	*The Defense of Poesy*; *Pride and Prejudice*; 'Of Parents and Children'; 'A Telephone Call'; 'Kit Bag'; 'The English Exam'
Language choices	'On Imitation'; 'Deeper Than Colour'; *Learning to Think*; *Scott and Amundsen*; Communicating Feelings in Poems; 'Captain Scott's Tomb'; 'In from the Cold...'

Table 2: Framework Objectives

Extract Title	Framework Objectives
Section 1 – You Just Don't Understand...	
Gender Speech Issues and Social Factors	S&L5, S&L7, S&L11,
'A Telephone Call'	TR16, W9, TR12
Pride and Prejudice	S&L7, R6, TR16, TR13
The Sheep Pig	S&L7, R6, TR16, TR13
US Navy Transcript	S&L5, S&L7, S&L11
'Things My Girlfriend and I Have Argued About'	S7L7, TR15, TW15
Communicating Feelings in Poems	TR16, W9, TR12
Section 2 – The Generation Gap	
'The Miller's Tale'	
Have The Men Had Enough?	S5, S15, TR6, TW1, TW2
Of Parents and Children	S7, S18, W5, W11, W10, TR15, TR16, TR19
The Winter's Tale	S14, R16, R17
Buffy the Vampire Slayer	TR6, TR17, TR10
Section 3 – On Being a Reader	
The Lonely Planet – Antarctica	
'Guidance for Visitors', International Association of Antarctica Tour Operators	
Atlas Travel	
Captain Scott's Diary – The Last March	TR9, TR10, S13, TR8, S9, TR4
'Captain Scott's Tomb', *Daily Mirror* (1913)	TR4
Scott and Amundsen	W8, TR7, S11, R9, TW15, TR6, TR11
Terra Incognita 'In from the Cold', *Observer Review*	TR6, TR11

Section 1
You Just Don't Understand...

*Tho' I walks with fifty 'ousemaids outer Chelsea to the
   Strand
An' they talks a lot o' lovin' but wot do they understand?*

Rudyard Kipling, 1865–1936

No language, but the language of the heart.

Alexander Pope, 1688–1744

The extracts in this section illustrate some of the different
ways in which males and females communicate – and
some of the problems this can cause.

Extract 1.1: *Gender Speech Issues and Social Factors*

This extract from a piece of research considers whether men and women talk differently, and challenges the stereotype that women talk more.

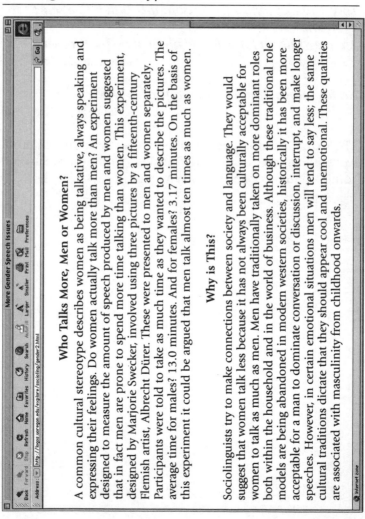

Who Talks More, Men or Women?

A common cultural stereotype describes women as being talkative, always speaking and expressing their feelings. Do women actually talk more than men? An experiment designed to measure the amount of speech produced by men and women suggested that in fact men are prone to spend more time talking than women. This experiment, designed by Marjorie Swecker, involved using three pictures by a fifteenth-century Flemish artist, Albrecht Dürer. These were presented to men and women separately. Participants were told to take as much time as they wanted to describe the pictures. The average time for males: 13.0 minutes. And for females? 3.17 minutes. On the basis of this experiment it could be argued that men talk almost ten times as much as women.

Why is This?

Sociolinguists try to make connections between society and language. They would suggest that women talk less because it has not always been culturally acceptable for women to talk as much as men. Men have traditionally taken on more dominant roles both within the household and in the world of business. Although these traditional role models are being abandoned in modern western societies, historically it has been more acceptable for a man to dominate conversation or discussion, interrupt, and make longer speeches. However, in certain emotional situations men will tend to say less; the same cultural traditions dictate that they should appear cool and unemotional. These qualities are associated with masculinity from childhood onwards.

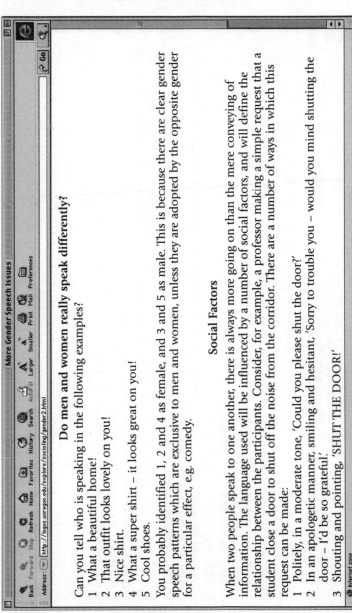

Address: http://logos.uoregon.edu/explore/socioling/gender3.html

Do men and women really speak differently?

Can you tell who is speaking in the following examples?

1 What a beautiful home!
2 That outfit looks lovely on you!
3 Nice shirt.
4 What a super shirt – it looks great on you!
5 Cool shoes.

You probably identified 1, 2 and 4 as female, and 3 and 5 as male. This is because there are clear gender speech patterns which are exclusive to men and women, unless they are adopted by the opposite gender for a particular effect, e.g. comedy.

Social Factors

When two people speak to one another, there is always more going on than the mere conveying of information. The language used will be influenced by a number of social factors, and will define the relationship between the participants. Consider, for example, a professor making a simple request that a student close a door to shut off the noise from the corridor. There are a number of ways in which this request can be made:

1 Politely, in a moderate tone, 'Could you please shut the door?'
2 In an apologetic manner, smiling and hesitant, 'Sorry to trouble you – would you mind shutting the door – I'd be so grateful.'
3 Shouting and pointing, 'SHUT THE DOOR!'

The most appropriate utterance would be 1, and the most inappropriate 3. The latter humiliates the student and shows disrespect. 2 is awkward because it implies that the professor is of a lower status than the student, but could also indicate shyness or low self-esteem.

When people settle on the right 'code' in their conversations, there are factors which come into play subconsciously.

- Participants – how well do they know each other?
- Social setting – is it formal or informal?
- Status of the participants in the conversations e.g. boss/employee; doctor/patient; student/professor.
- Aim or purpose of the conversation.
- Topic being discussed.

Do you notice differences in the way you speak to your friends, relatives, teachers and strangers? Automatically adjusting conversation to take account of differences is called selecting one's variety or code. Social and professional situations can be awkward when:

- There isn't agreement on the 'code'
- There is unfamiliarity with a particular 'code'.

Extract 1.2: 'A Telephone Call' by Dorothy Parker

This is written as an interior monologue – the thoughts passing through the girl's head as she waits for the phone to ring. It deals with the difficulty of people understanding each other in love relationships, or of expressing love.

Please, God, let him telephone me now. Dear God, let him call me now. I won't ask anything else of You, truly I won't. It isn't very much to ask. It would be so little to You, God, such a little, little thing. Only let him telephone now. Please, God. Please, please, please.

If I didn't think about it, maybe the telephone might ring. Sometimes it does that. If I could think of something else. If I could think of something else. Maybe if I counted five hundred by fives, it might ring by that time. I'll count slowly. I won't cheat. And if it rings when I get to three hundred, I won't stop; I won't answer it until I get to five hundred. Five, ten, fifteen, twenty, twenty-five, thirty, thirty-five, forty, forty-five, fifty... Oh, please ring. Please.

This is the last time I'll look at the clock. I will not look at it again. It's ten minutes past seven. He said he would telephone at five o'clock. 'I'll call you at five, darling.' I think that's where he said 'darling.' I'm almost sure he said it there. I know he called me 'darling' twice, and the other time was when he said goodbye. 'Goodbye, darling.' He was busy, and he can't say much in the office, but he called me 'darling' twice. He couldn't have minded my calling him up. I know you shouldn't keep telephoning them – I know they don't like that. When you do that, they know you are thinking about them and wanting them, and that makes them hate you. But I hadn't talked to him in three days – not in three days. And all I did was ask him how he was; it was just the way anybody might have called him up. He couldn't have minded that. He couldn't have thought I was bothering him. 'No, of course you're not,' he said. And he said he'd telephone me. He didn't have to say that. I didn't ask him to, truly I didn't. I'm sure I didn't. I don't think he would say he'd telephone me, and then just never do it. Please don't let him do that, God. Please don't.

'I'll call you at five, darling.' 'Goodbye, darling.' He was busy, and he was in a hurry, and there were people around him, but he called me 'darling' twice. That's mine, that's mine. I have that, even if I never see him again. Oh, but that's so little. That isn't enough. Nothing's enough, if I never see him again. Please let me see him again. God. Please, I want him so much. I want him so much. I'll be good, God. I will try to be better, I will, if You will let me see him again. If You let him telephone me. Oh, let him telephone me now.

Ah, don't let my prayer seem too little to You, God. You sit up there, so white and old, with all the angels about You and the stars slipping by. And I come to You with a prayer about a telephone call. Ah, don't laugh, God. You see, You don't know how it feels. You're so safe, there on Your throne, with the blue swirling under You. Nothing can touch You; no one can twist Your heart in his hands. This is suffering, God, this is bad, bad suffering. Won't You help me? For Your Son's sake, help me. You said You would do whatever was asked of You in His name. Oh, God, in the name of Thine only beloved Son, Jesus Christ, our Lord, let him telephone me now.

I must stop this. I mustn't be this way. Look. Suppose a young man says he'll call a girl up, and then something happens, and he doesn't. That isn't so terrible, is it? Why, it's going on all over the world, right this minute. Oh, what do I care what's going on all over the world? Why can't that telephone ring? Why can't it, why can't it?

Couldn't you ring? Ah, please, couldn't you? You damned, ugly, shiny thing. It would hurt you to ring, wouldn't it? Oh, that would hurt you. Damn you, I'll pull your filthy roots out of the wall, I'll smash your smug black face in little bits. Damn you to hell.

No, no, no. I must stop. I must think about something else. This is what I'll do. I'll put the clock in the other room. Then I can't look at it. If I do have to look at it, then I'll have to walk into the bedroom, and that will be something to do. Maybe, before I look at it again, he will call me. I'll be so sweet to him, if he calls me. If he says he can't see me tonight, I'll say, 'Why, that's all right, dear. Why, of course it's all right.' I'll be the way I was when I first met him. Then maybe he'll like me again. I was always sweet, at first. Oh, it's so easy to be sweet to people before you love them.

I think he must still like me a little. He couldn't have called me 'darling' twice today, if he didn't still like me a little. It isn't all gone, if he still likes me a little; even if it's only a little, little bit. You see, God, if You would just let him telephone me, I wouldn't have to ask You anything more. I would be sweet to him, I would be gay, I would be just the way I used to be, and then he would love me again. And then I would never have to ask You for anything more. Don't You see, God? So won't You please let him telephone me? Won't You please, please, please?

Are you punishing me, God, because I've been bad? Are You angry with me because I did that? Oh, but, God, there are so many bad people – You could not be hard only to me. And it wasn't very bad; it couldn't have been bad. We didn't hurt anybody, God. Things are only bad when they hurt people. We didn't hurt one single soul; You know that. You know it wasn't bad, don't You, God? So won't You let him telephone me now?

If he doesn't telephone me, I'll know God is angry with me. I'll count five hundred by fives, and if he hasn't called me then, I will know God isn't going to help me, ever again. That will be the sign. Five, ten, fifteen, twenty, twenty-five, thirty, thirty-five, forty, forty-five, fifty, fifty-five… It was bad. I knew it was bad. All right, God, send me to hell. You think You're frightening me with Your hell, don't You? You think Your hell is worse than mine.

I mustn't. I mustn't do this. Suppose he's a little late calling me up – that's nothing to get hysterical about. Maybe he isn't going to call – maybe he's coming straight up here without telephoning. He'll be cross if he sees I have been crying. They don't like you to cry. He doesn't cry. I wish to God I could make him cry. I wish I could make him cry and tread the floor and feel his heart heavy and big and festering in him. I wish I could hurt him like hell.

He doesn't wish that about me. I don't think he even knows how he makes me feel. I wish he could know, without my telling him. They don't like you to tell them they've made you cry. They don't like you to tell them you're unhappy because of them. If you do, they think you're possessive and exacting. And then they hate you. They hate you whenever you say anything you really think. You always have to keep playing little games. Oh, I thought we didn't have to; I thought this was so big I could say whatever I meant. I guess you can't, ever. I guess there isn't ever anything big enough for that. Oh, if he would just telephone. I wouldn't tell him I had been sad about him. They hate sad people. I would be so sweet and so gay, he couldn't help but like me. If he would only telephone. If he would only telephone.

Maybe that's what he is doing. Maybe he is coming on here without calling me up. Maybe he's on his way now. Something might have happened to him. No, nothing could ever happen to him. I can't picture anything happening to him. I never picture him run over. I never see him lying still and long and dead. I wish he were dead.

That's a terrible wish. That's a lovely wish. If he were dead, he would be mine. If he were dead, I would never think of now and the last few weeks. I would remember only the lovely times. It would be all beautiful. I wish he were dead. I wish he were dead, dead, dead.

This is silly. It's silly to go wishing people were dead just because they don't call you up the very minute they said they would. Maybe the clock's fast; I don't know whether it's right. Maybe he's hardly late at all. Anything could have made him a little late. Maybe he had to stay at his office. Maybe he went home, to call me up from there, and somebody came in. He doesn't like to telephone me in front of people. Maybe he's worried, just a little, little bit, about keeping me waiting. He might even hope that I would call him up. I could do that, I could telephone him.

I mustn't. I mustn't, I mustn't. Oh, God, please don't let me telephone him. Please keep me from doing that. I know, God, just as well as You do, that if he were worried about me, he'd telephone no matter where he was or how many people there were around him. Please make me know that, God. I don't ask You to make it easy for me – You can't do that, for all that You could make a world. Only let me know it, God. Don't let me go on hoping. Don't let me say comforting things to myself. Please don't let me hope, dear God. Please don't.

I won't telephone him. I'll never telephone him again as long as I live. He'll rot in hell, before I'll call him up. You don't have to give me strength, God; I have it myself. If he wanted me, he could get me. He knows where I am. He knows I'm waiting here. He's so sure of me, so sure. I wonder why they hate you as soon as they are sure of you. I should think it would be so sweet to be sure.

It would be so easy to telephone him. Then I'd know. Maybe it wouldn't be a foolish thing to do. Maybe he wouldn't mind. Maybe he'd like it. Maybe he has been trying to get me. Sometimes people try and try to get you on the telephone, and they say the number doesn't answer. I'm not just saying that to help myself; that really happens. You know that really happens, God. Oh, God, keep me away from that telephone. Keep me away. Let me still have just a little bit of pride. I think I'm going to need it, God. I think it will be all I'll have.

Oh, what does pride matter, when I can't stand it if I don't talk to him? Pride like that is such a silly, shabby little thing. The real pride, the big pride, is in having no pride. I'm not saying that just because I want to call him. I am not. That's true, I know that's true. I will be big. I will be beyond little prides.

Please, God, keep me from telephoning him. Please, God.

I don't see what pride has to do with it. This is such a little thing, for me to be bringing in pride, for me to be making such a fuss about. I may have misunderstood him. Maybe he said for me to call him up, at five. 'Call me at five, darling.' He could have said that, perfectly well. It's so possible that I didn't hear him right. 'Call me at five, darling.' I'm almost sure that's what he said. God, don't let me talk this way to myself. Make me know, please make me know.

I'll think about something else. I'll just sit quietly. If I could sit still. If I could sit still maybe I could read. Oh, all the books are about people who love each other, truly and sweetly. What do they want to write about that for? Don't they know it isn't true? Don't they know it's a lie, it's a God damned lie? What do they have to tell about that for, when they know how it hurts? Damn them, damn them, damn them.

I won't. I'll be quiet. This is nothing to get excited about. Look. Suppose he were someone I didn't know very well. Suppose he were another girl. Then I'd just telephone and say, 'Well, for goodness' sake, what happened to you?' That's what I'd do, and I'd never even think about it. Why can't I be casual and natural, just because I love him? I can be. Honestly, I can be. I'll call him up, and be so easy and pleasant. You see if I won't, God. Oh, don't let me call him. Don't, don't, don't.

God, aren't You really going to let him call me? Are You sure, God? Couldn't You please relent? Couldn't You? I don't even ask You to let him telephone me this minute, God: only let him do it in a little while. I'll count five hundred by fives. I'll do it so slowly and so fairly. If he hasn't telephoned then, I'll call him. I will. Oh, please, dear God, dear kind God, my blessed Father in Heaven, let him call before then. Please. God. Please.

Five, ten, fifteen, twenty, twenty-five, thirty, thirty-five...

Extract 1.3: *Pride and Prejudice* by Jane Austen

In this opening chapter, Jane Austen introduces Mr and Mrs Bennet, who have five single daughters. This was written at a time when marriage was the only real option for women of the gentry, and girls who couldn't bring a fortune to the altar were at a disadvantage.

Chapter 1

It is a truth universally acknowledged, that a single man in possession of a good fortune, must be in want of a wife.

However little known the feelings or views of such a man may be on his first entering a neighbourhood, this truth is so well fixed in the minds of the surrounding families, that he is considered as the rightful property of some one or other of their daughters.

'My dear Mr Bennet,' said his lady to him one day, 'have you heard that Netherfield Park is let at last?'

Mr Bennet replied that he had not.

'But it is,' returned she; 'for Mrs Long has just been here, and she told me all about it.'

Mr Bennet made no answer.

'Do not you want to know who has taken it?' cried his wife impatiently.

'*You* want to tell me, and I have no objection to hearing it.'

This was invitation enough.

'Why, my dear, you must know, Mrs Long says that Netherfield is taken by a young man of large fortune from the north of England; that he came down on Monday in a chaise and four to see the place, and was so much delighted with it that he agreed with Mr Morris immediately; that he is to take possession before Michaelmas, and some of his servants are to be in the house by the end of next week.'

'What is his name?'

'Bingley.'

'Is he married or single?'

'Oh! single, my dear, to be sure! A single man of large fortune; four or five thousand a year. What a fine thing for our girls!'

'How so? how can it affect them?'

'My dear Mr Bennet,' replied his wife, 'how can you be so tiresome! You must know that I am thinking of his marrying one of them.'

'Is that his design in settling here?'

'Design! Nonsense, how can you talk so! But it is very likely that his *may* fall in love with one of them, and therefore you must visit him as soon as he comes.'

'I see no occasion for that. You and the girls may go, or you may send them by themselves, which perhaps will be still better, for as you are as handsome as any of them, Mr Bingley might like you the best of the party.'

'My dear, you flatter me. I certainly *have* had my share of beauty, but I do not pretend to be anything extraordinary now. When a woman has five grown up daughters, she ought to give over thinking of her own beauty.'

'In such cases, a woman has not often much beauty to think of.'

'But, my dear, you must indeed go and see Mr Bingley when he comes into the neighbourhood.'

'It is more than I engage for, I assure you.'

'But consider your daughters. Only think what an establishment it would be for one of them. Sir William and Lady Lucas are determined to go, merely on that account, for in general you know they visit no new comers. Indeed you must go, for it will be impossible for us to visit him, if you do not.'

'You are over scrupulous surely. I dare say Mr Bingley will be very glad to see you; and I will send a few lines by you to assure him of my hearty consent to his marrying which ever he chuses of the girls; though I must throw in a good word for my little Lizzy.'

'I desire you will do no such thing. Lizzy is not a bit better than the others; and I am sure she is not half so handsome as Jane, nor half so good humoured as Lydia. But you are always giving *her* the preference.'

'They have none of them much to recommend them,' replied he; 'they are all silly and ignorant like other girls; but Lizzy has something more of quickness than her sisters.'

'Mr Bennet, how can you abuse your own children in such a way? You take delight in vexing me. You have no compassion on my poor nerves.'

'You mistake me, my dear. I have a high respect for your nerves. They are my old friends. I have heard you mention them with consideration these twenty years at least.'

'Ah! you do not know what I suffer.'

'But I hope you will get over it, and live to see many young men of four thousand a year come into the neighbourhood.'

'It will be no use to us, if twenty such should come since you will not visit them.'

'Depend upon it, my dear, that when there are twenty, I will visit them all.'

Mr Bennet was so odd a mixture of quick parts, sarcastic humour, reserve, and caprice, that the experience of three and twenty years had been insufficient to make his wife understand his character. *Her* mind was less difficult to develop. She was a woman of mean understanding, little information, and uncertain temper. When she was discontented she fancied herself nervous. The business of her life was to get her daughters married; its solace was visiting and news.

Extract 1.4: *The Sheep Pig* by Dick King Smith

In this opening of a well-known children's story, we can see Dick King Smith using similar techniques to Jane Austen to create first impressions of his characters and their relationship.

Chapter 1
'Guess my weight'

'What's that noise?' said Mrs Hogget, sticking her comfortable round red face out of the kitchen window. 'Listen, there 'tis again, did you hear it, what a racket, what a row, anybody'd think someone was being murdered, oh dearie me, whatever is it, just listen to it, will you?'

Farmer Hogget listened. From the usually quiet valley below the farm came a medley of sounds: the oompah oompah of a brass band, the shouts of children, the rattle and thump of a skittle alley, and every now and then a very high, very loud, very angry-sounding squealing lasting perhaps ten seconds.

Farmer Hogget pulled out an old pocket-watch as big round as a saucer and looked at it. 'Fair starts at two,' he said. 'It's started.'

'I knows that,' said Mrs Hogget, 'because I'm late now with all theseyer cakes and jams and pickles and preserves as is meant to be on the Produce Stall this very minute, and who's going to take them there, I'd like to know, why you are, but afore you does, what's that noise?'

The squealing sounded again.

'That noise?'

Mrs Hogget nodded a great many times. Everything that she did was done at great length, whether it was speaking or simply nodding her head. Farmer Hogget, on the other hand, never wasted his energies or his words.

'Pig,' he said.

Mrs Hogget nodded a lot more.

'I thought 'twas a pig, I said to meself that's a pig that is, only nobody round here do keep pigs, 'tis all sheep for miles about, what's a pig doing, I said to meself, anybody'd think they was killing the poor thing, have a look when you take all this stuff down, which you better do now, come and give us a hand, it can go in the back of the Land Rover, 'tisn't raining, 'twon't hurt, wipe your boots afore you comes in.'

'Yes,' said Farmer Hogget.

Extract 1.5: US Navy Transcript

This transcript is claimed to be of an actual radio conversation between a US Naval ship and the Canadians, off the coast of Newfoundland in October 1995.

CANADIANS:	Please divert your course 15 degrees to the South, to avoid a collision.
AMERICANS:	Recommend you divert your course 15 degrees to the North, to avoid a collision.
CANADIANS:	Negative. You will have to divert your course 15 degrees to the South to avoid a collision.
AMERICANS:	This is the Captain of a US Navy ship. I say again, divert YOUR course.
CANADIANS:	Negative. I say again, you will have to divert your course.
AMERICANS:	THIS IS THE AIRCRAFT CARRIER USS LINCOLN. THE SECOND LARGEST SHIP IN THE UNITED STATES ATLANTIC FLEET, WE ARE ACCOMPANIED BY THREE DESTROYERS, THREE CRUISERS, AND NUMEROUS SUPPORT VESSELS. I DEMAND THAT YOU CHANGE YOUR COURSE 15 DEGREES NORTH, I SAY AGAIN, THAT'S 15 DEGREES NORTH, OR COUNTERMEASURES WILL BE UNDERTAKEN TO ENSURE THE SAFETY OF THIS SHIP.
CANADIANS:	We are a lighthouse. Your call.

Extract 1.6: 'Things My Girlfriend and I Have Argued About' by Mil Millington

This extract is taken from Mil Millington's website and newspaper column and offers a light-hearted perspective of the ways in which men and women can misunderstand one another.

She keeps making me answer the phone. I'll be sitting watching the final fifteen seconds of a TV serial that I've been following for seven months (say), the phone will ring and she'll jut her head towards it and instruct 'Get that'. The thing about this is; we both know it will never, ever, ever, though-we-continue-till-the-Earth-spirals-down-into-the-sun, ever be for me. I've received perhaps three phone calls in the last eleven years, and that's counting people asking if I have a few moments to hear about an exciting new development in the area of index-linked pensions. Everyone I know either emails me or sends me dog excrement through the post, depending on the context. Margret, on the other hand, is legally obliged to have a phone clasped to the side of her head on her passport photo.

What's even more irritating, is that as I, inevitably, hand her the phone she'll hiss 'Who is it?' presumably to cut through that .04 of a second it would be before she finds out for herself. Oh, no, don't you go thinking it's because she might do the panic-faced, hand-waving 'Say I'm not in!' thing, oh, Lordy, no. Proof of this is that I always say 'Just leave the ansafone on – then you can hear who it is before you pick up.' But –

'Get that.'

'No need, the ansafone's on.'

– then, she always leaps towards the phone to pick up before the crucial fourth ring. And, incidentally, always fails. 'Hello, I . . . [great wail of feedback] Oh damn, the ['Hello, we can't get to . . . '] Hold on . . . [random hammering at buttons, 'the phone right now', feedback] Mil! Miiiiiiiiiiil! Stop this thing now!'

Oh, and while we're here, if I called my friend Mark to ask, for example, 'What time's the train tomorrow?' it'd go:

ME: Hi, Mark? What time's the train tomorrow?
MARK: It's 9.20, Mil.
ME: OK, cheers.
MARK: Bye.

If Margret calls a friend to ask 'What time's the train tomorrow?' it might come in a shade under three hours. If our house ever catches fire and Margret makes the call, then the embers will be cold by the time the fire brigade arrives. Though doubtless they'll all arrive knowing that Margret thinks 'not a dark colour for the bathroom because she feels it'll make it look small'.

Romance. I am far more romantic than Margret. This is a simple fact. Occasionally Margret will ask – out of the blue, we'll just be sitting together on the sofa, say – 'Do you love me?'. I'll reply 'What are you on about? I go out with you, don't I?'. Which, I think you can see, proves I'm more romantic than she is. My love is not some temporary thing that needs to be repeatedly stated lest it slips my mind; I have constancy. The fact that Margret invariably gets annoyed with my reply is because she hasn't thought her enquiry through; she's not sure what she means. Conversely, when I say to Margret 'Do you love me?', we're both perfectly clear that it means 'I've just bought myself a rather expensive piece of electrical equipment that you haven't seen yet'.

Extract 1.7: Communicating Feelings in Poems

Each of these poems deals with the difficulty of communicating feelings: wanting more to be said; being afraid to say how you feel; misunderstanding what is said; trying to find a way to express love.

'I Love You It's True'
by Carole Stewart

I love you it's true but is there anything in that?
I loved baked potatoes and cheese,
Nice ripe red tomatoes and salad cream.
But does that mean anything?
Our tastes change and then infatuation…
Boredom sets in
And I must try something new.
But I love you and I loved Curly-Wurlys,
Mars bars and Fry's Turkish Delight.
Now my sweet tooth is dead.
I love you it's true but is there anything in that?

'Unfortunate Coincidence'
by Dorothy Parker

By the time you swear you're his,
Shivering and sighing,
And he vows his passion is
Infinite, undying –
Lady make a note of this:
One of you is lying.

'I'm Really Very Fond'
by Alice Walker

I'm really very fond of you,
he said.

I don't like fond.
It sounds like something
you would tell a dog.

Give me love,
or nothing.

Throw your fond in a pond,
I said.

But what I felt for him
was also warm, frisky,
moist-mouthed,
eager,
and could swim away

if forced to do so.

Activities

Gender Speech Issues and Social Factors

1   Read through the extracts and think about these questions:

   a Do you think boys talk more than girls?

   b Might this vary with the situation? For example:
      - in mixed groups
      - in classrooms
      - in single sex groups
      - in social situations.

   c Are there differences in the ways in which boys and girls express themselves? For example, greetings – it has been observed that boys will often nod and greet by simply saying the person's name; girls may be more likely to say hello/hi/hiya.

   d What are the differences in the way we talk to different people, and what affects these? Think of:
      - a younger sibling
      - a friend
      - a teacher
      - parents.

2   Research projects:

   a Make a note of the different ways in which boys and girls greet their friends during the course of a day/ evening. If you are at a single sex or boarding school, make a note of how different social groups do this.

   b Using a stopwatch, time the talk of boys and girls in the classroom (get your teacher's permission first!). If you are at a single sex school, use a television or radio discussion programme as a focus.

c With permission, listen to the ways in which boys/girls or men/women talk on the telephone. Make a note of: gender of both people involved in call; length of conversation; affirmative comments which encourage the other person (e.g. *mmm*; *yeah*; *I know*). Compare the results for different genders. Using the same results, compare for other factors, e.g. age, nature of relationship.

d Record the ways in which your/your friends' speech changes during the course of a day according to the audience. What 'codes' are being used?

'A Telephone Call'

1 This is written as an interior monologue – the thoughts passing through the girl's head as she waits for the phone to ring. Why do you think Parker has chosen to do this?

2 Find examples that show how Parker:
   • suggests desperation
   • shows the girl can't think about anything else
   • blames herself
   • blames a higher power.

   Who *doesn't* she blame?

3 The girl endlessly tries to interpret what the man said to her. Find examples of:
   • what he said
   • how she tries to interpret it.

   Then write down what *you* think he probably meant.

4 Consider all the different things that 'I'll call you' can mean.

5 Try to identify the emotions being expressed in the different parts of the story, e.g. hope, despair, powerlessness, anger, guilt, etc. Create a graph or timeline to represent these.

6 Look at the ending. Is it an ending? What is being suggested?

Pride and Prejudice

1 Read the text again. This chapter is carefully structured and has a lot of work to do. In it, Austen has to:

• establish the main themes of the novel

• establish characters and relationships

• entertain and interest the reader.

You are going to explore some of the ways in which she does this, and look particularly at her use of dialogue.

2 Look at the opening sentence.

a What does it establish as the theme of the novel?

b How does it help to place the family socially?

c Is it a 'truth'? If not, what does this ironic opening suggest about i) Jane Austen's views? ii) a possible moral of the novel?

3 Now look at the dialogue between Mr and Mrs Bennet.

a Compare the length of their speeches.

b Mr Bennet's words are often in *reported* speech, and Mrs Bennet's in *direct* speech. Why do you think Austen has done this? What does it suggest about the two characters and their relationship?

c Look at Mrs Bennet's use of exclamations, and at the sort of detail that makes up most of her speeches. What is Austen showing us about her?

d Find all the examples that you can where Mr Bennet is teasing his wife, but she takes him seriously. What impression does this convey?

e Think about the fact that *you* know when Mr Bennet is not serious but *she* doesn't. Which character are we expected to have most sympathy with? How are we supposed to regard Mrs Bennet?

4 The family:

    a Look at the comments Mr and Mrs Bennet make about their daughters. What does this show about their values/attitudes?

    b How does it set up tension/expectations for later?

5 The closing: Read the final paragraph again. Think of all the impressions you have formed so far. What is Austen doing here before her reader moves on to the rest of the story?

6 As a group, discuss how far the conversation between the couple is typical of male and female speech patterns.

7 Comparison: Read the opening of *The Sheep Pig* by Dick King Smith. Using your findings from this work, explore the similarities in structure and technique.

US Navy Transcript

Look at the radio transcript.

1 What style of language is being used here and why?

2 Within this style, who is attempting to express power and how? How is this represented through:

    a vocabulary

    b the way this transcript has been typed out?

3 Who actually has the power and why? How is this expressed?

'Things My Girlfriend and I Have Argued About'

1 Look again at the text. Using your notes from the previous extracts, find examples here that show:

- the different ways in which men and women talk
- the difficulty men and women can have understanding each other

- the irritation that can build up in long term relationships
- the author sharing mockery of one of the characters with the reader.

2   Compare the attitude in 'Things . . .' to that in *High Fidelity* (page 166). Can you find differences or similarities? Is there a sense in which both men know they are in the wrong? How is this conveyed to the reader?

Communicating Feelings in Poems

1   **a**   Write down as many statements as you can starting with 'I love'. Group them according to meaning/seriousness.

  b   Arrange these phrases in a line according to seriousness:

    I love
    I like
    I am fond of
    I am in love with
    I am besotted with
    I am committed to

2   Look at the three poems: 'I Love You It's True' by Carole Stewart; 'Unfortunate Coincidence' by Dorothy Parker; 'I'm Really Very Fond' by Alice Walker. Each of these poems deals with the difficulty of communicating feelings:

- wanting more to be said
- being afraid to say how you feel
- misunderstanding what is said
- trying to find a way to express love.

3 In groups, read through and discuss the selection then
take a poem each. Create a poster based on your poem,
with the poem pasted into the middle of a larger sheet.
On your poster highlight and comment on:

- interesting words
- interesting images
- the structure of the poem
- interesting use of sound/rhythm/rhyme
- how love is expressed
- difficulties in expressing love
- the poet's attitude/the poem's message
- and any other features you want to comment on.

Use illustrations/images from magazines, etc. to
represent the ideas and images you find.

4 Present your poster to the rest of the group/class.
Compare and discuss the posters each group has made.

Section 2
The Generation Gap

I would there were no age between sixteen and three-and-twenty, or that youth would sleep out the rest; for there is nothing in the between but getting wenches with child, wronging the ancientry, stealing, fighting –

William Shakespeare,
The Winter's Tale, Act 3, Scene III

For youth and elde is often at debaat.

Geoffrey Chaucer,
'The Miller's Tale', Canterbury Tales

The extracts in this section explore some different and sometimes unexpected angles of a very old issue…

Extract 2.1: 'The Miller's Tale' from *The Canterbury Tales* by Geoffrey Chaucer

In Chaucer's time, poetry was read aloud or spoken. It was important to keep audience interest alive through a strong rhythm and rhyme scheme, which helped sustain pace.

Heere bigynneth the Millere his Tale

     Whilom ther was dwellynge at Oxenford
80   A riche gnof, that gestes heeld to bord,
     And of his craft he was a carpenter.
     With hym ther was dwellynge a poure scoler,
     Hadde lerned art, but al his fantasye
     Was turned for to lerne astrologye,
85   And koude a certeyn of conclusiouns,
     To demen by interrogaciouns,
     If that men asked hym in certain houres
     Whan that men sholde have droghte or elles
       shoures,
     Or if men asked hym what sholde bifalle
90   Of every thyng; I may nat rekene hem alle.
     This clerk was cleped hende Nicholas.
     Of deerne love he koude and of solas;
     And therto he was sleigh and ful privee,
     And lyk a mayden meke for to see.
95   A chambre hadde he in that hostelrye
     Allone, withouten any compaignye,
     Ful fetisly ydight with herbes swoote;
     And he hymself as sweete as is the roote
     Of lycorys, or any cetewale.
100 His Almageste, and bookes grete and smale,
     His astrelabie, longynge for his art,
     His augrym stones layen faire apart,

On shelves couched at his beddes heed;
His presse ycovered with a faldyng reed

105   And al above ther lay a gay sautrie,
On which he made a-nyghtes melodie
So swetely that all the chambre rong;
And Angelus ad virginem he song;
And after that he song the Kynges Noote.

110   Ful often blessed was his myrie throte.
And thus this sweete clerk his tyme spente
After his freendes fyndyng and his rente.
This carpenter hadde new a wyf,
Which that he lovede moore than his lyf;

115   Of eighteteene yeer she was of age.
Jalous he was, and heeld hire narwe in cage,
For she was wylde and yong, and he was old,
And demed hymself, been lik a cokewold.
He knew nat Catoun, for his wit was rude,

120   That bad man sholde wedde his simylitude.
Men sholde wedden after hire estaat,
For youth and elde is often at debaat.
But sith that he was fallen in the snare,
Her moste endure, as oother folk, his care.

125   Fair was this yonge wyf, and therwithal
As any wezele hir body gent and smal.
A ceynt she werede, barred al of silk,
A barmclooth as whit as morne milk
Upon her lendes, ful of many a goore.

130   Whit was hir smok, and broyden al bifoore
And eek bihynde, on hir coler aboute,
Of col-blak silk, withinne and eek withoute.
The tapes of hir white voluper
Were of the same suyte of his coler;

135   Hir filet brood of silk, and set ful hye.
And sikerly she hadde a likerous ye;
Ful smale ypulled were hire browes two,

And tho were bent and blake as any sloo.
She was ful moore blisful on to see
140   Than is the newe pere-jonette tree,
And softer than the wolle is of a wether.
And by hir girdel heeng a purs of lether,
Tasseled with silk, and perled with latoun.
In all this world, so seken up and doun,
145   There nys no man so wys that koude thenche
So gay a popelote or swich a wenche.
Ful brighter was the shynyng of hir hewe
Than in the Tour the noble yforged newe.
But of hir song, it was as loude and yerne
150   As any swalwe sittynge on a berne.
Therto she koude skippe and make game,
As any kyde or calf folwynge his dame.
Hir mouth was sweete as bragot or the meeth,
Or hoord of apples leyd in hey or heeth.
155   Wynsynge she was, as is a joly colt,
Long as a mast, and upright as a bolt.
A brooch she baar upon hir lowe coler,
As brood as is the boos of a bokeler.
Hir shoes were laced on hir legges hye.
160   She was a prymerole, a piggesnye,
For any lord to leggen in his bedde,
Or yet for any good yeman to wedde.

Extract 2.2: *Have the Men Had Enough?* by Margaret Forster

This passage deals with three generations, and describes the difficulties of coping with a grandparent with dementia.

Have the men had enough?
Never mind the men.
Which men?
Hurry up, the potatoes will be cold.
I'd love a potato.
Then take one, Grandma.
Have the men had enough?

Always the same. Every week, every Sunday. All of us crowded round the table, Grandma wedged in between Bridget and Paula, Bridget of course laughing at everything Grandma says and Paula not even smiling, and moving away, ever so slightly, when Grandma plonks a hand flat in the gravy as she searches for her fork.

Have the men had enough?
Yes, thank you, Mother.
Who's Mother?
You are, go on, Mother, help yourself.
Hold the plate steady.
Steady the Buffs.
Go *on*, Grandma.
Have the men had enough?

Always the same. Dad desperate to fill his face, but patient, good-humoured, coaxing Grandma along and Adrian impatient, resenting the ritual when he's just in from football and starving and not disposed to care about Grandma's feelings, as dear Bridget well knows so she drags it out and encourages Grandma to peer round the table and fuss on until eventually Mum calls a halt and piles her plate and then it starts, the next little song, the next refrain:

Pass the salt.
Grandma, everything's covered in salt.
It's salty enough.
Salt's bad for you.
It hardens the arteries.
Hers have been silted up for years.
Adrian!
Pass the salt.

Who does it irritate more? Hard to say. Mum long ago stopped seeing this passion for salt as an insult to her cooking, in fact I think it gives her a kind of malicious pleasure to watch Grandma totally ruin the food, watch her covering the delicate slices of delicious herb-scattered chicken, the crisp roasted potatoes, the bright green leeks (Grandma loves leeks but not the way Mum does them, barely tossed in lemon and butter, she likes the hell boiled out of them), covering all of it heavily with salt.

Pass the salt.
It's in front of you.
Stick it in her hand.
Stick it in her mouth.
Adrian!
It'll ruin her taste-buds.
She hasn't got any.
Pass the salt.

Finally, when the salt has fallen like scurf, Grandma is satisfied. She eats, with her hands. Paula concentrating hard on her own plate, Bridget cooing and praising and expertly pushing the potatoes out of the gravy, and we all hurry to eat before the inevitable, before Grandma says the chicken is tough, which of course it isn't but who can bother saying this when it's melting in all our mouths that very minute, and then she takes her bottom teeth out (the top set are already out, lost sometime between breakfast and lunch and likely to turn up in any place from the peg basket to the biscuit tin). She uses them as a scoop, grating them through the shallows of the gravy to fish out a potato, and Adrian laughs and Dad smiles and Mum moves her face not a muscle and Paula closes her eyes and Bridget snatches the teeth, rushes to the sink, rams them back into Grandma's mouth.

Any pudding?
You haven't finished your lovely dinner.
Throw it in the waste bin for God's sake.
Hannah!
Give it to me, come on.
Adrian!
Any pudding?

Bridget takes a bit of the chicken, all cold and ruined by the gravy which only Grandma has because she won't eat anything not sodden with thick, dark gravy, and Adrian leans across and spears the potatoes knocking aside Dad, who is grappling for one of the drier ones, and Mum removes the plate and plonks down in front of Grandma a bowl of her very special absolutely beautiful apple trifle, which takes half a pint of double cream, a certain sort of apple, sponge which Mum makes herself and loads of time to concoct and we adore it. She puts extra cream on to make it even more sloppy for poor Grandma's gums. The spoon is put in Grandma's hand but since she is likely just to shove her mit straight in the cream and begin a plastering job on her face, Bridget has arranged a napkin under her chin. Bridget oohs and aahs and keeps telling Grandma, 'You Are Certainly Going To Enjoy This Mum,' and praising my own Mum for making it, reminding Grandma that Jenny has made it specially for her. Grandma takes one mouthful and we brace ourselves and, yes, she spits it out, face contorted with disgust, miserable with disappointment.

It's sour!
Mum, it is not.
Put some sugar on for her.
It's drowned in sugar.
Just give her straight sugar.
Adrian!
It's sour!

Mum already has it taken away and passed on to Dad who couldn't give tuppence that Grandma, is spitting it out, has spat into the bowl and flecks of saliva are spotting the cream. Mum substitutes a bowl of ice cream, chocolate, with chocolate sauce, heavily sweetened, on top of it. Grandma says it's lovely and begins applying it to every crevice of her skin but getting a good deal down the hatch too. Bridget watches her adoringly, pleased she is quiet and content at last. It's nearly over, the weekly ordeal, the worst of all similar ordeals in the week. We all relax. After the main course we all have a salad before the pudding, a huge green salad with a garlicky dressing. Grandma does not usually want salad but doesn't like to be left out so Mum makes sure that she goes through the motions of serving Grandma who sometimes takes a bit of green pepper or a sliver of celery and plays with it, but not today; today she most graciously declines and says so clearly that she has had an excellent sufficiency that we all laugh, nicely. Only one more ritual to go.

Has anyone a cigarette?
Not yet, Mother, we're still eating.
Have it with your tea, Grandma.
Wait till I've left the room.
Charlie!
It's her only pleasure, Charlie.
Has anyone a cigarette?

That marks the end, really, unless anyone is foolish enough to have dallied over their salad and not got on to the pudding. Dad takes his with him, not at all put out by Bridget's reprimand. Bridget of course smokes, as does Paula actually, surprisingly, so she naturally doesn't mind Grandma filling our house with smoke. Mum hates it but ostentatiously holds her peace, knowing that Dad's protest is enough. Well, he does get bronchitis often – smoke is bad for him. Adrian has already gone out. He disapproves of smoking, being your sporty health-freak type. We can do without his self-righteousness. Paula has left the table and sits in a corner of the kitchen, thoughtfully opening the window beside her before she has her own cigarette. Grandma shivers melodramatically and announces darkly that there is a draught from somewhere and Bridget, who stays at the table to smoke companionably with her, covers her shoulders with a tartan shawl. She doesn't bother turning to look at Paula. Paula isn't really a smoker – it's seventy-five per cent letting the cigarette burn and only a few puffs. But Bridget – wow. It's quite frightening, the intensity, the sheer power of the deep drags, the apparent absolute disappearance of the smoke. I used to think she was a magician: I'd get all excited about where it went and Dad would say it wasn't a trick, that some nice little containers called lungs collected it and that if Bridget could take them out and look at them she'd find they were covered in tar. It was all beyond me, especially as Grandma, quite sharp then, would immediately protect Bridget from her mean brother and say either A Little Of What You Fancy Does You Good or There Is No Harm In It. Bridget is an addict. If she can't find her cigarettes it's pitiful to see her. She is frantic, unhinged, almost hysterical. Now, Grandma is never like that. She's an elegant smoker which, for a woman lacking elegance in any other way, is odd. She has good hands, long-fingered, narrow-palmed, and a pretty way of holding a cigarette. Bridget talks with a cigarette in her mouth. I've even seen her drink with it there, but Grandma never does. She smokes slowly, knocks ash off neatly, is relaxed. Bridget is right: it is, next to tea, her one remaining pleasure. And she has the tea now, a big yellow pot of it, strong and dark, though she says repeatedly she hates strong tea. Once, Mum believed her and prepared her finest Darjeeling, poured it into a sweet little rosebud-covered cup. Grandma almost had a fit at the 'coloured water'. Weak tea to Mum is half a pint of water to one tea bag and strong is a whole tea bag in a cup. Weak to Grandma is a whole tea bag in a cup and strong is six in half a pint of water. In her mug – Grandma is only comfortable with large workmen's mugs – there are three heaped teaspoons of sugar. It is fascinating to watch three more go in, be languidly stirred, tasted, smiled over.

Then Mum helps her up and I take the other side and Grandma is so happy to be half-cuddled between us that she does a little dance as we walk through to the living room and Dad says that's a good Highland Fling and Grandma says she thinks she'll go to the Highlands. We lower her onto the sofa and she asks us to mind her legs, which are sore, then Mum puts a pillow at her head and I fetch her the crocheted blanket, crocheted by Grandma in her heyday, a lovely thing in violent colours, and Grandma sighs and says it's nice to get up in the morning but it's nicer to stay in your bed. She closes her eyes. The

match starts with a roar. Grandma says that men and their
football are the very devil and the dirty boots and the
filthy clothes and is the water heated ready and men must
work and women must weep. She's asleep. Mum dashes
for her coat and runs through instructions while she puts
it on: Keep her covered, remind her about the loo when
she wakens, only one more cup of tea or she'll wet the
bed and Mildred will give up. Dad grunts. Mum goes.

And I am here, in my room, wondering. What I want to
know is:

Why don't more people kill themselves when they get
   old?
Why do relatives not kill old people more?
What is the point of keeping old people alive anyway?
Haven't the women had enough, as well as the men?
Will somebody please tell me?

Extract 2.3: 'Of Parents and Children' by Francis Bacon

Francis Bacon wrote a series of essays early in the seventeenth century to inform and advise people. Some of what he says may ring true today; other parts may show how much attitudes have changed.

Essay VII

The joys of parents are secret, and so are their griefs and fears: they cannot utter the one, nor they will not utter the other. Children sweeten labours, but they make misfortunes more bitter: they increase the cares of life, but they mitigate the remembrance of death. The perpetuity by generation is common to beasts; but memory, merit and noble works are proper to men: and surely a man shall see the noblest works and foundations have proceeded from childless men, which have sought to express the images of their minds, where those of their bodies have failed: so the care of posterity is most in them that have no posterity. They that are the first raisers of their houses are most indulgent towards their children; beholding them as the continuance not only of their kind but of their work; and so both children and creatures.

The difference in affection of parents towards their several children is many times unequal, and sometimes unworthy, especially in the mother; as Salomon saith, *A wise son rejoiceth the father, but an ungracious son shames the mother*. A man shall see, where there is a house full of children, one or two of the eldest respected, and the youngest made wantons; but in the midst some that are as it were forgotten, who many times nevertheless prove the best. The illiberality of parents in allowance towards their children is an harmful error; makes them base; acquaints them with shifts; makes them sort with mean company; and makes them surfeit more when they come to plenty: and therefore the proof is best, when men keep their authority towards their children, but not their purse. Men have a foolish manner (both parents and schoolmasters and servants) in creating and breeding an emulation between brothers during childhood, which many times sorteth to discord when they are men, and disturbeth families. The Italians make little difference between children and nephews or near kinsfolks; but so they be of the lump, they care not though they pass not through their own body. And, to say truth, in nature it is much a like matter; insomuch that we see a nephew sometimes resembleth an uncle or a kinsman more than his own parent; as the blood happens. Let parents choose betimes the vocations and courses they mean their children should take; for then they are most flexible; and let them not too much apply themselves to the disposition of their children, as thinking they will take best to that which they have most mind to. It is true, that if the affection or aptness of the children be extraordinary, then it is good not to cross it; but generally the precept is good, *Optimum elige, suave et facile illud faciet consuetudo*. Younger brothers are commonly fortunate, but seldom or never where the elder are disinherited.

Extract 2.4: *The Winter's Tale* by William Shakespeare

In this extract, Prince Florizel, disguised as a country youth, is about to make a binding oath to marry Perdita, a shepherdess. Unknown to him, his father, King Polixenes (also in disguise) has come to prevent it. Shakespeare shows us the rage of the controlling, autocratic parent and the hot-headed impulsiveness of the youth in love. (There is a happy ending, by the way: Perdita turns out to be a Princess-in-disguise, naturally!)

Act Four, Scene Four

SHEPHERD   Take hands, a bargain!
And, friends unknown, you shall bear witness
   to 't:
I give my daughter to him, and will make
Her portion equal his.

FLORIZEL   O, that must be
I' the virtue of your daugher: one being dead,
I shall have more than you can dream of yet;
Enough then for your wonder. But, come on,
Contract us 'fore these witnesses.

SHEPHERD   Come, your hand;
And, daughter, yours.

POLIXENES   Soft, swain, awhile, beseech you;
Have you a father?

FLORIZEL   I have: but what of him?

POLIXENES   Knows he of this?

FLORIZEL   He neither does nor shall.

POLIXENES   Methinks a father
Is at the nuptial of his son a guest
That best becomes the table. Pray you once
   more,

Is not your father grown incapable
Of reasonable affairs? is he not stupid
With age and altering rheums? can he speak? hear?
Know man from man? dispute his own estate?
Lies he not bed-rid? and again does nothing
But what he did being childish?

FLORIZEL No, good sir;
He has his health and ampler strength indeed
Than most have of his age.

POLIXENES By my white beard,
You offer him, if this be so, a wrong
Something unfilial: reason my son
Should choose himself a wife, but as good reason
The father, all whose joy is nothing else
But fair posterity, should hold some counsel
In such a business.

FLORIZEL I yield all this;
But for some other reasons, my grave sir,
Which 'tis not fit you know, I not acquaint
My father of this business.

POLIXENES Let him know't.

FLORIZEL He shall not.

POLIXENES Prithee, let him.

FLORIZEL No, he must not.

SHEPHERD Let him, my son: he shall not need to grieve
At knowing of thy choice.

FLORIZEL Come, come, he must not.
Mark our contract.

POLIXENES Mark your divorce, young sir,

(Discovering himself)

Whom son I dare not call; thou art too base
To be acknowledged: thou a sceptre's heir,
That thus affect'st a sheep-hook! Thou old
    traitor,
I am sorry that by hanging thee I can
But shorten thy life one week. And thou,
    fresh piece
Of excellent witchcraft, who of force must know
The royal fool thou copest with, –

SHEPHERD　O, my heart!

POLIXENES　I'll have thy beauty scratch'd with briers, and
    made
More homely than thy state. For thee, fond boy,
If I may ever know thou dost but sigh
That thou no more shalt see this knack, as never
I mean thou shalt, we'll bar thee from
    succession;
Not hold thee of our blood, no, not our kin,
Far than Deucalion off: mark thou my words:
Follow us to the court. Thou churl, for this
    time,
Though full of our displeasure, yet we free
    thee
From the dead blow of it. And you,
    enchantment. –
Worthy enough a herdsman: yea, him too,
That makes himself, but for our honour
    therein,
Unworthy thee, – if ever henceforth thou
These rural latches to his entrance open,
Or hoop his body more with thy embraces,
I will devise a death as cruel for thee
As thou art tender to't.

Exit

PERDITA   Even here undone!
I was not much afeard; for once or twice
I was about to speak and tell him plainly,
The selfsame sun that shines upon his court
Hides not his visage from our cottage but
Looks on alike. Will't please you, sir, be gone?
I told you what would come of this: beseech
    you,
Of your own state take care: this dream of
    mine, –
Being now awake, I'll queen it no inch
    farther,
But milk my ewes and weep.

CAMILLO   Why, how now, father!
Speak ere thou diest.

SHEPHERD   I cannot speak, nor think
Nor dare to know that which I know. O sir!
You have undone a man of fourscore three,
That thought to fill his grave in quiet, yea,
To die upon the bed my father died,
To lie close by his honest bones: but now
Some hangman must put on my shroud and
    lay me
Where no priest shovels in dust. O cursed
    wretch,
That knew'st this was the prince,
and wouldst adventure
To mingle faith with him! Undone! undone!
If I might die within this hour, I have lived
To die when I desire.

Exit

FLORIZEL   Why look you so upon me?

I am but sorry, not afeard; delay'd,
But nothing alter'd: what I was, I am;
More straining on for plucking back, not
    following
My leash unwillingly.

CAMILLO   Gracious my lord,
You know your father's temper: at this time
He will allow no speech, which I do guess
You do not purpose to him; and as hardly
Will he endure your sight as yet, I fear:
Then, till the fury of his highness settle,
Come not before him.

FLORIZEL   I not purpose it.
I think, Camillo?

CAMILLO   Even he, my lord.

PERDITA   How often have I told you 'twould be thus!
How often said, my dignity would last
But till 'twere known!

FLORIZEL   It cannot fail but by
The violation of my faith; and then
Let nature crush the sides o' the earth together
And mar the seeds within! Lift up thy looks:
From my succession wipe me, father; I
Am heir to my affection.

CAMILLO   Be advised.

FLORIZEL   I am, and by my fancy: if my reason
Will thereto be obedient, I have reason;
If not, my senses, better pleased with madness,
Do bid it welcome.

CAMILLO   This is desperate, sir.

FLORIZEL   So call it: but it does fulfil my vow;
I needs must think it honesty. Camillo,
Not for Bohemia, nor the pomp that may

Be thereat glean'd, for all the sun sees or
The close earth wombs or the profound sea hides
In unknown fathoms, will I break my oath
To this my fair beloved: therefore, I pray you,
As you have ever been my father's honour'd friend,
When he shall miss me, – as, in faith, I mean not
To see him any more, – cast your good counsels
Upon his passion; let myself and fortune
Tug for the time to come. This you may know
And so deliver, I am put to sea
With her whom here I cannot hold on shore;
And most opportune to our need I have
A vessel rides fast by, but not prepared
For this design. What course I mean to hold
Shall nothing benefit your knowledge, nor
Concern me the reporting.

CAMILLO   O my lord!
I would your spirit were easier for advice,
Or stronger for your need.

Extract 2.5: *Buffy the Vampire Slayer* by Joss Whedon

This is one of the scenes from 'Band Candy' (Season 3).
In this episode of the cult teen-gothic show, all the adults
start to behave like teenagers after eating mysterious
candy bars.

Int. Science classroom – the next day

*A science classroom, with two-person tables.
The students wait for the teacher. Buffy and
Cordelia share a table. Xander and Willow
have the table behind them.*

CORDELIA　I heard there's this secret rule if a
teacher is over ten minutes late,
everyone can leave.

BUFFY　It's Giles' turn to lead study hall. He'll
be here. He's allergic to late.

CORDELIA　The man is wrapped a little tight. I
had this philosophy book out from
the library for like a year and he made
me pay the fine even though it was
huge. I eventually had to return it,
which was sad because it was perfect
for starting conversations with college
boys. Of course, that was B.X.

BUFFY　B.X.? Oh, Before Xander. Clever.

CORDELIA　Where is Giles already? I'm bored and
he's not here to give me credit for it.

ANGLE: PRINCIPAL SNYDER

*And an older teacher, Ms Barton, are engaged
in a whispered conversation in the classroom
doorway. Snyder is eating a Band Candy Bar.*

PRINCIPAL SNYDER   Look, the big pinhead librarian didn't show up and I don't want to do it. You do it.

MS BARTON   All right. Fine. I'll do it.

She moves to the front of the room, and Snyder heads out.

PRINCIPAL SNYDER   *(to himself)*
Everyone expects me to do everything around here 'cause I'm the principal and it's not fair . . .

Snyder exits. The students continue to chatter.

MS BARTON   *(very tough)*
Hey, hey!

The students look up, startled.

MS BARTON   Look, we're all stuck here, okay? So let's just sit quietly . . . *(lowering her voice)* and pretend to read or something until we're sure Commandant Snyder is gone, and then we're all out of here.

The students look at each other, happy and surprised.

XANDER   Anyone else want to marry Ms Barton?

CORDELIA   Get in line.

Ms Barton sets down her purse.

ANGLE: THE PURSE
No one notices the Band Candy Bar sticking out of it.

WILLOW   I guess Giles isn't coming.

BUFFY   *(concerned)*
        I guess not.

Int. The Bronze – evening (night)

The joint is jumping: packed and very loud. Buffy enters. Willow follows, still shaky from the ride.

Dingoes ate my babies *plays and looks out at an unusually old audience. Oz waves at Willow and gives a little shrug. Everywhere they look, the patrons are adults: at the bar, on the dance floor. The teenagers in the place are reacting pretty much the same as Buffy and Willow – staring in confusion.*

BUFFY   Whoa. Let's do the time warp again.

WILLOW   Maybe there's some kind of reunion in town or a Billy Joel tour or something.

A woman pushes past them. Buffy recognises her.

BUFFY   Ms Barton?

It is her. She blinks owlishly at Buffy, trying to focus.

MS BARTON   Buffy? Whoa.

WILLOW   You okay, Ms Barton?

MS BARTON   I'm cool, Willow. Willow. That's a tree. You're a tree. Do they have nachos here, little tree?

Ms Barton starts to laugh, a little out of control.

BUFFY   I think maybe you need some fresh air.

MS BARTON	Okay.

She amiably drifts off toward the door. Buffy and Willow watch her go.

WILLOW	Okay, this is not normal.

(off Buffy's look)

Maybe that goes without saying.

GUY'S VOICE	*(O.S.)* Hey, gang!

Buffy and Willow turn, probably expecting to see Xander. Instead:

PRINCIPAL SNYDER	*(continuing)* This place is fun city, huh?
BUFFY	Principal Snyder?
PRINCIPAL SNYDER	Call me Snyder. Just a last name. Like Barbarino. Whoo! I'm stoked! Did you see Ms Barton? I think she's wasted. I'm gonna put that on her next performance review because I'm the principal.

The music falters for a second. They turn and look.

ANGLE: THE STAGE
A shirtless pudgy adult dives off the stage, hooting and hollering. He is almost caught, but the out-of-shape men beneath him aren't up to it. He ends up on the floor, and gets to his feet slowly. A lot of the men are red-faced, sweaty, panting.

ANGLE: WILLOW AND BUFFY

WILLOW	I don't like this. They could have heart attacks.

BUFFY   Maybe there's a doctor here.

WILLOW   Actually, that is my doctor. He's usually less… topless.

PRINCIPAL SNYDER   I got a commendation. For being principal. From the mayor. He shook my hand twice.

A clique of three or four middle-aged women scurry past, laughing and shrieking.

PRINCIPAL SNYDER   Ooh. There's some foxy ladies here tonight!

WILLOW   *(to Buffy)*
               Buffy, what's happening?

BUFFY   I don't know, but it's happening to a whole lotta grownups.

WILLOW   They're acting like a bunch of…

BUFFY   They're acting like a bunch of us.

A beat, as the two girls look worriedly around them.

WILLOW   I don't act like this…

Int. the Bronze – night

Things are even wilder than they were a minute ago. The band has given up entirely. Oz stands with Buffy and Willow.

BUFFY   Something's changing them.

WILLOW   A spell?

OZ   They're teenagers. Sobering mirror to look into, huh?

PRINCIPAL SNYDER   *(to Oz)*
               You've got great hair.

Activities

'The Miller's Tale' from *The Canterbury Tales*

1   Read the tale aloud in the group. While you are doing this, listen for words that may *sound* familiar even if they look strange on the page. Make a note of what you think they mean.

   a   Divide the extract up into roughly equal sections to share between the group. Each member of the group will write a modern English version of their part of the tale. For this, you will need copies of this tale or the *Canterbury Tales* with a glossary of Middle English words in the back. Ask your English teacher or the school librarian – or you can follow the link from the Heinemann website (www.heinemann.co.uk/hotlinks).

   b   As you are translating your section of the text, make a list of the most unusual words. Then compile a chart with these headings:

Chaucer	Modern English	French	German	Latin

   You are going to see if you can trace the roots of the unfamiliar words. To do this you will need to borrow French, German and Latin dictionaries from the library or the Languages department.

   c   Create a poster of the word roots you have traced.

   d   Put together all the translated sections to form your own modern edition of the tale.

2   In Chaucer's time, poetry was read aloud or spoken. It was important to keep audience interest alive through a strong rhythm and rhyme scheme, which helped sustain pace.

a For a real challenge, work out the rule for the metre of Chaucer's original and try to make your modern version the same.

b The very ambitious may like to make it rhyme too!

3 Consider Chaucer's presentation of characters. In what ways are the two portraits that follow stereotypes? How far do these still hold true today?

Alison – the young wife	**Nicholas** – the student lodger
Find examples from the text which show:	Find examples from the text which show:
• Alison being described through her looks • Links with nature/ animals • Alison's flirtatious nature.	• Nicholas' main interests • How Nicholas spends his time.

4 Audience expectation: Think of the set-up in the carpenter's household, then consider lines 113–122 which describe the marriage.

a What moral about youth and age is given?

b What expectations has Chaucer set up and why do you think he has done this?

5 Chaucer the film director: Look again at the portrait of Alison. Compile a flow-chart to follow how the focus of the writing moves.

a How is this like a modern director's technique when suggesting a woman is desirable? Can you think of any examples from films/TV/adverts you have seen? Can you think of any examples of men being presented in this way?

b Media extension: Collect some front covers of magazines showing men or women. Which are shown doing things (described through action) and which are shown as passive attractive objects (described through appearance)? What links can you make with portraits of Nicholas and Alison?

Have the Men Had Enough?

1 Look at the way the chapter is set out. Certain parts of the dialogue are not presented in the usual way for direct speech, but as statements and responses in a church service (ask your head of RE for a service book to have a look at and compare). Why do you think Forster has chosen to do this?

2 This passage is written in the present tense. What effect does it have? To compare, choose a short passage and write it out in the past tense. What differences do you notice?

3 This part of the book is written in the first person, from the point of view of Hannah, the teenage daughter. Find examples of the writing that suggest she:

- is a keen observer of detail
- uses language typical of an internal conversation
- knows and understands family relationships well
- is sensitive to tensions.

Why are these elements important to the reader?

4 Reading for implied meaning: Try to work out where Hannah's sympathies lie, through examining her descriptions of the others and their behaviour. Try to describe how sympathy or irritation are suggested.

5 Part of the tension here seems to emerge from class differences as well as age. Explore the ways in which these are suggested through manners, activities and tastes.

6   Creative writing: Using the stylistic features you have noticed in this piece as a model, try writing a ritualised description of something that happens regularly in your own life – it could be registration, getting home from school each day, a nightly telephone call to a friend/family member. This could be a real or imagined situation.

Of Parents and Children

1   Attitudes: Read through the essay. Create a chart in your book with these headings:

True today	Seventeenth-century attitude	Reflected in other extracts

Now complete the table with quotations/brief explanations for each heading. In the third one, you will have to look carefully at your notes on the other extracts in this section. You may have to draw out/infer the general point that is being made about parents and children in the writing. You will probably find it helpful to discuss this with a partner. You can use extracts from elsewhere in *Thoughtlines* too.

2   Language change: Try to work out the meaning of these words and phrases from the context, and use a dictionary if you get stuck. Note that some of these words are commonly used today, but have a different sort of meaning here:

> labours   illiberality   wantons   surfeit   emulation
> vocations   affection   aptness   kinsfolks

3   a   Style: Bacon is famed for the quality of his writing. Some people even believe that he actually wrote Shakespeare's plays. You are going to look at some of the features of his style that make his prose memorable. See if you can find examples of the following.

- Contrast and balance – find sentences expressing two contrasted ideas in their clauses.
- Structure – find examples of structures that give an equal balance to sentences e.g.: *not only… but also* or *many times… some times*.
- Repetition or listing for effect.
- Alliteration, especially of related verbs or related adjectives in sentences.

b Try reading parts aloud in groups or pairs. What effect do these stylistic features have when the writing is heard? Why might this have been important in the 1600s?

c Now try creating some sentences of your own using some of the same structures. You could try, on your own or in a pair, to write a parody of Bacon on, for example, teachers and students, dogs and their owners, etc.

The Winter's Tale

1 Read this scene carefully. Consider the ways in which the scene from *The Winter's Tale* is made dramatic.

a The audience has more knowledge of the situation than some of the characters on stage have. The earlier part of the play ensures the audience knows that the stranger in disguise at Prince Florizel's betrothal to a shepherd's daughter is, in fact, his father King Polixenes. Borrow a copy of *The Winter's Tale* from your school library and read the first part of the play, then look again at the extract. How does Shakespeare use the audience's superior knowledge of what is really going on to build tension and drama in this scene? Find an example where you think this works well.

b In this scene, the father, Polixenes, makes extreme threats. Find examples of these and make a list. Look at the language he uses. How genuine do you think he is? Why do you think Shakespeare makes his character utter these words? Consider the effect they have on the other characters, and the audience.

c Look at how Florizel responds to his parent. How does Shakespeare create sympathy for him? Can you identify any similarities between father and son?

d Now read the other characters' responses to the father carefully. How do their comments affect the audience's view of Polixenes' behaviour?

2 Drama activity: Create a mime version of the scene, using movement, gesture and expression to build tension and drama.

3 Media activity: Create a storyboard which uses camera angle and types of shot to convey emotions, power in relationships and key dramatic moments.

4 To think about: You will encounter other plays by Shakespeare in your school career. Many of his works feature dispute between the generations as a central theme or plot device. For example, *Romeo and Juliet*, *King Lear*, *As You Like It*, *A Midsummer Night's Dream*, *Hamlet* and *The Merchant of Venice* all contain dispute and breakdown in the relationships between parents and children. When you read further plays, keep your work on these extracts in mind, and look out for similar concerns and dramatic techniques.

Buffy the Vampire Slayer

1 Read through the scenes. You are going to look at the ways in which Whedon suggests that the adults have become teenagers.

a How do they talk?

b What attitudes and moods do they express?

2 Looking at stage directions:

   a How does Whedon reinforce the idea that the adults have become teenagers through the action described?

   b How is it hinted that the candy bars might be responsible?

3 Humour:

   a Whedon makes the adults use slang that was current when they themselves were young – what effect does this have on the real teenagers/a teenage television audience?

   b How is visual comedy created?

4 Stereotypes:

   a Compare Whedon's switching of stereotypes here with Forster's in the extract from *Have the Men Had Enough?* What similarities/differences can you find?

5 Final comment: Look at Oz's statement 'Sobering mirror to look into, huh?'. What does he mean by this? Do you think Whedon gives a true picture of teenage behaviour in the adults who have eaten the 'Band Candy'?

Section 3
On Being a Reader

We came to probe the Antarctic's mystery, to reduce this land in terms of science, but there is always the indefinable which holds aloof yet which rivets our souls.

Douglas Mawson

The truth is rarely pure, and never simple.

Oscar Wilde, 1854–1900

In this section, you are going to look at how writers can create very different impressions of the same places or events through their use of language, detail, fact and opinion.

Extract 3.1: The Lonely Planet – Antarctica

The Lonely Planet gives a range of information about distant places; their geography and culture. This extract is taken from the National Geographic website which featured the Lonely Planet perspective of Antarctica.

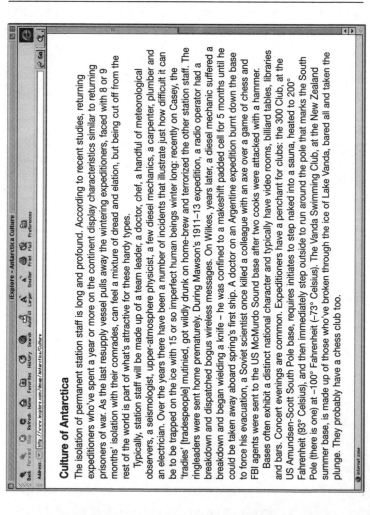

Culture of Antarctica

The isolation of permanent station staff is long and profound. According to recent studies, returning expeditioners who've spent a year or more on the continent display characteristics similar to returning prisoners of war. As the last resupply vessel pulls away the wintering expeditioners, faced with 8 or 9 months' isolation with their comrades, can feel a mixture of dread and elation, but being cut off from the rest of the world is part of what's attractive for these hardy types.

Typically, station staff will be made up of a team leader, a doctor, chef, a handful of meteorological observers, a seismologist, upper-atmosphere physicist, a few diesel mechanics, a carpenter, plumber and an electrician. Over the years there have been a number of incidents that illustrate just how difficult it can be to be trapped on the ice with 15 or so imperfect human beings winter long: recently on Casey, the 'tradies' [tradespeople] mutinied, got wildly drunk on home-brew and terrorized the other station staff. The ringleaders were sent home prematurely. During Mawson's 1911–13 expedition, a radio operator had a breakdown and dispatched bogus wireless messages. On Wilkes, years later, a diesel mechanic suffered a breakdown and began wielding a knife – he was confined to a makeshift padded cell for 5 months until he could be taken away aboard spring's first ship. A doctor on an Argentine expedition burnt down the base to force his evacuation, a Soviet scientist once killed a colleague with an axe over a game of chess and FBI agents were sent to the US McMurdo Sound base after two cooks were attacked with a hammer.

Bases often exhibit a distinct national character and typically have video rooms, billiard tables, libraries and bars. Concert evenings are common. Expeditioners have a penchant for clubs: the 300 Club, at the US Amundsen-Scott South Pole base, requires initiates to step naked into a sauna, heated to 200° Fahrenheit (93° Celsius), and then immediately step outside to run around the pole that marks the South Pole (there is one) at –100° Fahrenheit (–73° Celsius). The Vanda Swimming Club, at the New Zealand summer base, is made up of those who've broken through the ice of Lake Vanda, bared all and taken the plunge. They probably have a chess club too.

iExplore – Antarctica Culture

Address: http://www.iexplore.com/dmap/Antarctica/Culture

There are no indigenous peoples of Antarctica, but that doesn't mean that visitors shouldn't be respectful of fragile societies that do exist there. Antarctic bases are places of work and researchers need to take time out of their work to accommodate tourists. There's a desire amongst the Antarctic communities to be hospitable to visitors, but they are often pressed for time to complete their work before the season ends. Never enter any building unless you're specifically invited – you may interfere with scientific work or invade someone's privacy, a precious thing in a crowded base. Always take your shoes or boots off when you enter a station building – 90 tourists trudging mud into a base can take a long time to clean up. Never ask to use the toilet in a base: it's environmentally unsound to leave your waste on Antarctica when the facilities on your ship are available, and the onerous task of emptying or cleaning the toilet on the base is made all the worse when a bunch of unthinking tourists fill it to the brim. Perform your ablutions before you leave the ship.

Activities

For the most part, Antarctic tourists come to walk around, look at the scientific bases, take some photographs and journey out on zodiacs to the region's spectacular sights. Increasingly, however, tour operators are offering more for the outdoorsy type who's skied, climbed, camped and trekked everywhere else and wants a new challenge, and the demand seems to be there. People wishing to camp ashore must bring their own sleeping bags and foam mats, and climbers must supply their own crampons, ice axes and harnesses.

For the first time, scuba diving, including night diving, is being offered to tourists who have suitable qualifications. No decompression diving is undertaken – the dives are less than 39m (128ft). All divers must have at least 100 logged dives and be certified as a PADI Rescue Diver or higher (equivalent qualifications are accepted). Divers must bring all their own equipment.

In 1995, more than 100 runners participated in the first Antarctic Marathon run over a 42km (26 mile) double-loop course on King George Island in the South Shetlands, and the race was a near disaster. The runners started at the Uruguayan base of Artigas and passed through Russian, Chilean and Chinese stations and included some highly dangerous and unsupervised sections. Some of the participants became delirious with hypothermia, others were lost in the fog on top of a glacier and one fell into a crevasse up to his chest. Despite this and the heavy criticism that event drew the organizers are keen to run the marathon again.

Internet zone

Extract 3.2: 'Guidance for Visitors', International Association of Antarctica Tour Operators

IAATO is a member organization founded in 1991 to advocate, promote and practise safe and environmentally responsible private-sector travel to the Antarctic. The following extract is intended as a guide for people planning to visit the Antarctic.

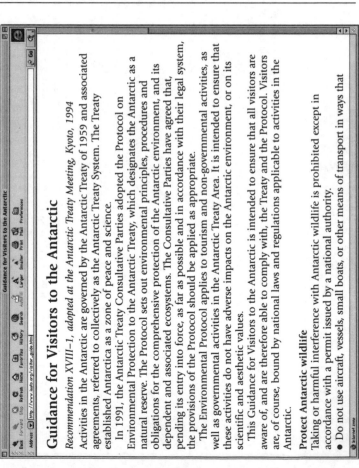

Guidance for Visitors to the Antarctic

Recommendation XVIII–1, adopted at the Antarctic Treaty Meeting, Kyoto, 1994

Activities in the Antarctic are governed by the Antarctic Treaty of 1959 and associated agreements, referred to collectively as the Antarctic Treaty System. The Treaty established Antarctica as a zone of peace and science.

In 1991, the Antarctic Treaty Consultative Parties adopted the Protocol on Environmental Protection to the Antarctic Treaty, which designates the Antarctic as a natural reserve. The Protocol sets out environmental principles, procedures and obligations for the comprehensive protection of the Antarctic environment, and its dependent and associated ecosystems. The Consultative Parties have agreed that, pending its entry into force, as far as possible and in accordance with their legal system, the provisions of the Protocol should be applied as appropriate.

The Environmental Protocol applies to tourism and non-governmental activities, as well as governmental activities in the Antarctic Treaty Area. It is intended to ensure that these activities do not have adverse impacts on the Antarctic environment, or on its scientific and aesthetic values.

This Guidance for Visitors to the Antarctic is intended to ensure that all visitors are aware of, and are therefore able to comply with, the Treaty and the Protocol. Visitors are, of course, bound by national laws and regulations applicable to activities in the Antarctic.

Protect Antarctic wildlife

Taking or harmful interference with Antarctic wildlife is prohibited except in accordance with a permit issued by a national authority.

● Do not use aircraft, vessels, small boats, or other means of transport in ways that

Guidance for Visitors to the Antarctic

Address: http://www.iaato.org/visitor_guide.htm

disturb wildlife, either at sea or on land.

- Do not feed, touch, or handle birds or seals, or approach or photograph them in ways that cause them to alter their behavior. Special care is needed when animals are breeding or molting.
- Do not damage plants, for example by walking, driving, or landing on extensive moss beds or lichen-covered scree slopes.
- Do not use guns or explosives. Keep noise to the minimum to avoid frightening wildlife.
- Do not bring non-native plants or animals into the Antarctic such as live poultry, pet dogs and cats or house plants.

Respect protected areas

A variety of areas in the Antarctic have been afforded special protection because of their particular ecological, scientific, historic or other values. Entry into certain areas may be prohibited except in accordance with a permit issued by an appropriate national authority. Activities in and near designated Historic Sites and Monuments and certain other areas may be subject to special restrictions.

- Know the locations of areas that have been afforded special protection and any restrictions regarding entry and activities that can be carried out in and near them.
- Observe applicable restrictions.
- Do not damage, remove, or destroy Historic Sites or Monuments or any artefacts associated with them.

Respect scientific research

- Do not interfere with scientific research, facilities or equipment.
- Obtain permission before visiting Antarctic science and support facilities; reconfirm arrangements 24–72 hours before arrival; and comply with the rules regarding such visits.
- Do not interfere with, or remove, scientific equipment or marker posts, and do not disturb experimental study sites, field camps or supplies.

Internet zone

Guidance for Visitors to the Antarctic

Address: http://www.iaato.org/visitor_guide.html

Be safe

Be prepared for severe and changeable weather and ensure that your equipment and clothing meet Antarctic standards. Remember that the Antarctic environment is inhospitable, unpredictable, and potentially dangerous.

- Know your capabilities, the dangers posed by the Antarctic environment, and act accordingly. Plan activities with safety in mind at all times.
- Keep a safe distance from all wildlife, both on land and at sea.
- Take note of, and act on, the advice and instructions from your leaders; do not stray from your group.
- Do not walk onto glaciers or large snow fields without the proper equipment and experience; there is a real danger of falling into hidden crevasses.
- Do not expect a rescue service. Self-sufficiency is increased and risks reduced by sound planning, quality equipment, and trained personnel.
- Do not enter emergency refuges (except in emergencies). If you use equipment or food from a refuge, inform the nearest research station or national authority once the emergency is over.
- Respect any smoking restrictions, particularly around buildings, and take great care to safeguard against the danger of fire. This is a real hazard in the dry environment of Antarctica.

Keep Antarctica pristine

Antarctica remains relatively pristine, the largest wilderness area on Earth. It has not yet been subjected to large-scale human perturbations. Please keep it that way.

- Do not dispose of litter or garbage on land. Open burning is prohibited.
- Do not disturb or pollute lakes or streams. Any materials discarded at sea must be disposed of properly.
- Do not paint or engrave names or graffiti on rocks or buildings.
- Do not collect or take away biological or geological specimens or man-made artefacts as a souvenir, including rocks, bones, eggs, fossils, and parts or contents of buildings.
- Do not deface or vandalize buildings, whether occupied, abandoned, or unoccupied, or emergency refuges.

Internet zone

Extract 3.3: Atlas Travel

This extract is taken from a holiday company whose main concern is to sell the wonders of the Antarctic to tourists.

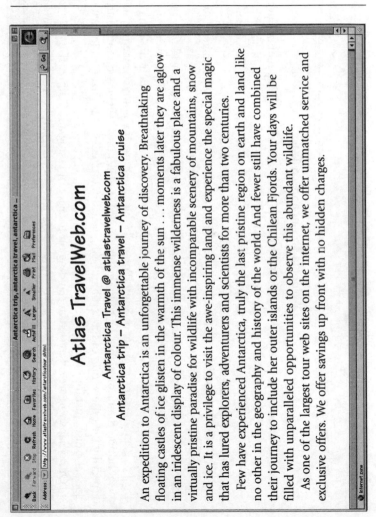

Atlas TravelWeb.com

Antarctica Travel @ atlastravelweb.com
Antarctica trip – Antarctica travel – Antarctica cruise

An expedition to Antarctica is an unforgettable journey of discovery. Breathtaking floating castles of ice glisten in the warmth of the sun . . . moments later they are aglow in an iridescent display of colour. This immense wilderness is a fabulous place and a virtually pristine paradise for wildlife with incomparable scenery of mountains, snow and ice. It is a privilege to visit the awe-inspiring land and experience the special magic that has lured explorers, adventurers and scientists for more than two centuries.

Few have experienced Antarctica, truly the last pristine region on earth and land like no other in the geography and history of the world. And fewer still have combined their journey to include her outer islands or the Chilean Fjords. Your days will be filled with unparalleled opportunities to observe this abundant wildlife.

As one of the largest tour web sites on the internet, we offer unmatched service and exclusive offers. We offer savings up front with no hidden charges.

Address: http://www.antarcticatravel.com/

Welcome to Antarctica Travel!

We are glad you are here. Like the great Antarctic explorer Sir Ernest Shackleton once said: 'Men go out into the void spaces of the world for various reasons. Some have the keen thirst for knowledge, and others are drawn away from the trodden path by the "lure of little voices", the mysterious fascination of the unknown.'

Let us help you discover the Earth's last unspoiled frontier. We offer a wide range of Antarctic adventures for all age and skill levels. You can travel to Antarctica with us by cruise ship from Argentina or Chile, or by icebreaker from Australia or New Zealand. Travelers with less time can fly by jet over Antarctica from Australia for a full day of aerial sightseeing. While most of our clients prefer to cruise Antarctica, for the truly adventurous we can arrange your Antarctic scuba diving, kayaking, mountain climbing, or South Pole trekking adventure. If you tour Antarctica and its neighboring chains of islands by ship, the whale, seal, and sea bird watching opportunities – especially the observation of Emperor and King Penguin rookeries – are first rate. In fact, we have special cruises just for birdwatchers.

Or perhaps you are interested in standing on pack ice or taking a helicopter flyover? Or maybe you'd prefer to observe spectacular icebergs and glaciers? We have 'em! For cruises to Antarctica, our

Internet zone

ships include the 450-passenger *MV Marco Polo*, smaller ships such as the *MS Hanseatic*, *MV Clipper Adventurer*, *World Discoverer*, *Caledonian Star*, and the *Explorer*; small ships such as the 49-passenger *Professor Multanovskiy*, and icebreakers such as the *Kapitan Dranitsyn* and *Kapitan Khlebnikov*.

Our Itineraries page provides cruise departure dates and tour destinations, fares, ship descriptions, and links to deck plans, daily cruise itineraries, and ship pictures. Our News page provides information on discounted Antarctic cruises. Our Antarctica page provides information on many of the cruise destinations. At Antarctica Travel, we are experts in making your expedition and cruise travel experiences to Antarctica among your fondest memories.

Contact us if you need a quote, further details, or to request one of our brochures.

Extract 3.4: *Captain Scott's Diary – The Last March*

Captain Scott and his companions died on an expedition to the South Pole. They reached the Pole, only to find that a Norwegian team had beaten them. On the return journey, already weak and hungry, tragedy struck...

Saturday, February 17. – A very terrible day. Evans looked a little better after a good sleep, and declared, as he always did, that he was quite well. He started in his place on the traces, but half an hour later worked his ski shoes adrift, and had to leave the sledge. The surface was awful, the soft recently fallen snow clogging the ski and runners at every step, the sledge groaning, the sky overcast, and the land hazy. We stopped after about one hour, and Evans came up again, but very slowly. Half an hour later he dropped out again on the same plea. He asked Bowers to lend him a piece of string. I cautioned him to come on as quickly as he could and he answered cheerfully as I thought. We had to push on, and the remainder of us were forced to pull very hard, sweating heavily. Abreast the Monument Rock we stopped, and seeing Evans a long way astern, I camped for lunch. There was no alarm at first, and we prepared tea and our own meal, consuming the latter. After lunch, and Evans still not appearing, we looked out, to see him afar off. By this time we were alarmed, and all four started back on ski. I was first to reach the poor man and shocked at his appearance; he was on his knees with clothing disarranged, hands uncovered and frost-bitten, and a wild look in his eyes. Asked what was the matter, he replied with a slow speech that he didn't know, but thought he must have fainted. We got him on his feet, but after two or three steps he sank down again. He showed every sign of complete collapse. Wilson, Bowers and I went back for the sledge, whilst Oates remained with him. When we returned he was practically unconscious, and when we got him into the tent quite comatose. He died quietly at 12.30 a.m. On discussing the symptoms we think he began to get weaker just before we reached the Pole, and that his downward path was accelerated first by the shock of his frost-bitten fingers, and later by falls during rough travelling on the glacier, further by his loss of all confidence in himself. Wilson thinks it certain he must have injured his brain by a fall. It is a terrible thing to lose a companion in this way, but calm reflection shows that there could not have been a better ending to the terrible anxieties of the past week. Discussion of the situation at lunch yesterday shows us what a desperate pass we were in with a sick man on our hands so far from home.

Friday, March 2. – Lunch. Misfortunes rarely come singly. We marched to the [Middle Barrier] depot fairly easily yesterday afternoon, and since that have suffered three distinct blows which have placed us in a bad position. First we found a shortage of oil. Second, Titus Oates disclosed his feet, the toes showing very bad indeed, evidently bitten by the late temperatures. The third blow came in the night, when the wind, which we had hailed with some joy, brought dark overcast weather. It fell below −40° in the night, and this morning it took $1\frac{1}{2}$ hours to get our foot-gear on. Worse was to come – the surface is simply awful. In spite of strong wind and full sail we have only done $5\frac{1}{2}$ miles. We are in a very queer street, since there is no doubt we cannot do the extra marches and feel the cold horribly.

Sunday, March 4. – Lunch. Things looking very black indeed. All the morning we had to pull with all our strength, and in $4\frac{1}{2}$ hours we covered $3\frac{1}{2}$ miles. Last night it was overcast and thick, surface bad; this morning sun shining and surface as bad as ever. We are about 42 miles from the next depot and have a week's food, but only about 3 to 4 days' fuel. We are in a very tight place indeed, but none of us despondent *yet*, or at least we preserve every semblance of good cheer, but one's heart sinks as the sledge stops dead at some sastrugi behind which the surface sand lies thickly heaped. For the moment the temperature is in the −20°, an improvement which makes us much more comfortable, but a colder snap is bound to come again soon. I fear that Oates at least will weather such an event very poorly. Providence to our aid! We can expect little from man now except the possibility of extra food at the next depot. It will be real bad if we get there and find the same shortage of oil. Shall we get there? Such a short distance it would have appeared to us on the summit! I don't know what I should do if Wilson and Bowers weren't so determinedly cheerful over things.

Monday, March 5. – Lunch. Regret to say going from bad to worse. We got a slant of wind yesterday afternoon, and going on 5 hours we converted our wretched morning run of 3½ miles into something over 9. We went to bed on a cup of cocoa and pemmican solid with the chill off. (R. 47.) The result is telling on all, but mainly on Oates, whose feet are in a wretched condition. One swelled up tremendously last night and he is very lame this morning. Sledge capsized twice; we pulled on foot, covering about 5½ miles. We are two pony marches and 4 miles about from our depot. Our fuel dreadfully low and the poor Soldier nearly done. It is pathetic enough because we can do nothing for him; more hot food might do a little, but only a little, I fear. We none of us expected these terribly low temperatures, and of the rest of us Wilson is feeling them most; mainly, I fear, from his self-sacrificing devotion in doctoring Oates' feet. We cannot help each other, each has enough to do to take

care of himself. The others, all of them, are unendingly
cheerful when in the tent. We mean to see the game through
with a proper spirit, but it's tough work to be pulling
harder than we ever pulled in our lives for long hours, and
to feel that the progress is so slow. One can only say 'God
help us!' and plod on our weary way, cold and very
miserable, though outwardly cheerful.

Wednesday, March 7. – A little worse, I fear. One of Oates'
feet *very* bad this morning; he is wonderfully brave. We still
talk of what we will do together at home.

We only made 6½ miles yesterday. This morning in
4½ hours we did just over 4 miles. We are 16 from our
depot. If we only find the correct proportion of food
there and this surface continues, we may get to the next
depot [Mt Hooper, 72 miles farther] but not to One Ton
Camp. We hope against hope that the dogs have been to
Mt Hooper; then we might pull through. If there is a
shortage of oil again we can have little hope. One feels
that for poor Oates the crisis is near, but none of us are
improving, though we are wonderfully fit considering the
really excessive work we are doing. We are only kept going
by good food. No wind this morning till a chill northerly air
came ahead. Sun bright and cairns showing up well. I should
like to keep the track to the end.

Sunday, March 11. – Titus Oates is very near the end, one
feels. What we or he will do, God only knows. We discussed
the matter after breakfast; he is a brave fine fellow and
understands the situation, but he practically asked for
advice. Nothing could be said but to urge him to march as
long as he could. One satisfactory result to the discussion;
I practically ordered Wilson to hand over the means of
ending our troubles to us, so that any one of us may know
how to do so. Wilson had no choice between doing so and

our ransacking the medicine case. We have 30 opium tabloids apiece and he is left with a tube of morphine. So far the tragical side of our story.

Monday, March 12. – We did 6.9 miles yesterday, under our necessary average. Things are left much the same, Oates not pulling much, and now with hands as well as feet pretty well useless. We did 4 miles this morning in 4 hours 20 min. – we may hope for 3 this afternoon, $7 \times 6 = 42$. We shall be 47 miles from the depot. I doubt if we can possibly do it. The surface remains awful, the cold intense, and our physical condition running down. God help us! Not a breath of favourable wind for more than a week, and apparently [we are] liable to head winds at any moment.

Friday, March 16, or Saturday 17. – Lost track of dates, but think the last correct. Tragedy all along the line. At lunch, the day before yesterday, poor Titus Oates said he couldn't go on; he proposed we should leave him in his sleeping-bag. That we could not do, and we induced him to come on, on the afternoon march. In spite of its awful nature for him he struggled on and we made a few miles. At night he was worse and we knew the end had come.

Should this be found I want these facts recorded. Oates' last thoughts were of his Mother, but immediately before he took pride in thinking that his regiment would be pleased with the bold way in which he met his death. We can testify to his bravery. He has borne intense suffering for weeks without complaint, and to the very last was able and willing to discuss outside subjects. He did not – would not – give up hope till the very end. He was a brave soul. This was the end. He slept through the night before last, hoping not to wake; but he woke in the morning – yesterday. It was blowing a blizzard. He said, 'I am just going outside and may be some time.' He went out into the blizzard and we have not seen him since.

I take this opportunity of saying that we have stuck to our sick companions to the last. In case of Edgar Evans, when absolutely out of food and he lay insensible, the safety of the remainder seemed to demand his abandonment, but Providence mercifully removed him at this critical moment. He died a natural death, and we did not leave him till two hours after his death. We knew that poor Oates was walking to his death, but though we tried to dissuade him, we knew it was the act of a brave man and an English gentleman. We all hope to meet the end with a similar spirit, and assuredly the end is not far.

I can only write at lunch and then only occasionally. The cold is intense, −40° at midday. My companions are unendingly cheerful, but we are all on the verge of serious frost-bites, and though we constantly talk of fetching through, I don't think any one of us believes it in his heart.

We are cold on the march now, and at all times except meals. Yesterday we had to lie up for a blizzard and today we move dreadfully slowly. We are at No. 14 pony camp, only two pony marches from One Ton Depot. We leave here our theodolite, a camera, and Oates' sleeping-bags. Diaries, etc., and geological specimens carried at Wilson's special request, will be found with us or on our sledge.

Sunday, March 18. − Today, lunch, we are 21 miles from the depot. Ill fortune presses, but better may come. We have had more wind and drift from ahead yesterday; had to stop marching; wind N.W., force 4, temp. −35°. No human being could face it, and we are worn out *nearly*.

The others are still confident of getting through − or pretend to be − don't know! We have the last *half* fill of oil in our primus and a very small quantity of spirit − this alone between us and thirst. The wind is fair for the moment, and that is perhaps a fact to help. The mileage would have seemed ridiculously small on our outward journey.

Wednesday, March 21. – Got within 11 miles of depot Monday night; had to lie up all yesterday in severe blizzard. Today forlorn hope, Wilson and Bowers going to depot for fuel.

22 and 23. – Blizzard bad as ever – Wilson and Bowers unable to start – tomorrow last chance – no fuel and only one or two of food left – must be near the end. Have decided it shall be natural – we shall march for the depot with or without our effects and die in our tracks.

[Thursday] March 29. – Since the 21st we have had a continuous gale from W.S.W. and S.W. We had fuel to make two cups of tea apiece and bare food for two days on the 20th. Every day we have been ready to start for our depot 11 miles away, but outside the door of the tent it remains a scene of whirling drift. I do not think we can hope for any better things now. We shall stick it out to the end, but we are getting weaker, of course, and the end cannot be far.

It seems a pity, but I do not think I can write more –

R. Scott

Last entry. For God's sake look after our people.

Message to the Public

The causes of the disaster are not due to faulty organization but to misfortune in all risks which had to be undertaken.

1 The loss of pony transport in March 1911 obliged me to start later than I had intended, and obliged the limits of stuff transported to be narrowed.
2 The weather throughout the outward journey, and especially the long gale in 83° S., stopped us.

3 The soft snow in lower reaches of glacier again
reduced pace.

We fought these untoward events with a will and
conquered, but it cut into our provision reserve.

Every detail of our food supplies, clothing and depots
made on the interior ice-sheet and over that long stretch
of 700 miles to the Pole and back, worked out to
perfection. The advance party would have returned to the
glacier in fine form and with surplus of food, but for the
astonishing failure of the man whom we had least expected
to fail. Edgar Evans was thought the strongest man of the
party.

The Beardmore Glacier is not difficult in fine weather,
but on our return we did not get a single completely fine
day; this with a sick companion enormously increased our
anxieties.

As I have said elsewhere, we got into frightfully rough
ice and Edgar Evans received a concussion of the brain –
he died a natural death, but left us a shaken party with the
season unduly advanced.

But all the facts above enumerated were as nothing to
the surprise which awaited us on the Barrier. I maintain
that our arrangements for returning were quite adequate,
and that no one in the world would have expected the
temperatures and surfaces which we encountered at this
time of the year. On the summit in lat. 85°, 86° we had −20°,
−30°. On the Barrier in lat. 82°, 10,000 feet lower, we had
−30° in the day, −47° at night pretty regularly, with
continuous head wind during our day marches. It is clear
that these circumstances came on very suddenly, and our
wreck is certainly due to this sudden advent of severe
weather, which does not seem to have any satisfactory
cause. I do not think human beings ever came through such
a month as we have come through, and we should have got
through in spite of the weather but for the sickening of a

second companion, Captain Oates, and a shortage of fuel in our depots for which I cannot account, and finally, but for the storm which has fallen on us within 11 miles of the depot at which we hoped to secure our final supplies. Surely misfortune could scarcely have exceeded this last blow. We arrived within 11 miles of our old One Ton Camp with fuel for one last meal and food for two days. For four days we have been unable to leave the tent – the gale howling about us. We are weak, writing is difficult, but for my own sake I do not regret this journey, which has shown that Englishmen can endure hardships, help one another, and meet death with as great a fortitude as ever in the past. We took risks, we knew we took them; things have come out against us, and therefore we have no cause for complaint, but bow to the will of Providence, determined still to do our best to the last. But if we have been willing to give our lives to this enterprise, which is for the honour of our country, I appeal to our countrymen to see that those who depend on us are properly cared for.

Had we lived, I should have had a tale to tell of the hardihood, endurance, and courage of my companions which would have stirred the heart of every Englishman. These rough notes and our dead bodies must tell the tale, but surely, surely, a great rich country like ours will see that those who are dependent on us are properly provided for.

R. Scott

Extract 3.5: 'Captain Scott's Tomb', *The Daily Mirror*

This newspaper story shows us how Scott and his team were regarded when the news of their deaths first broke. It shows us how attitudes, as well as language, have changed.

CAPTAIN SCOTT'S TOMB NEAR THE SOUTH POLE.

The Daily Mirror

24 Pages

THE MORNING JOURNAL WITH THE SECOND LARGEST NET SALE.

No. 2987.   Registered at the G.P.O. as a Newspaper.   WEDNESDAY, MAY 21, 1913   One Halfpenny.

THE MOST WONDERFUL MONUMENT IN THE WORLD: CAPTAIN SCOTT'S SEPULCHRE ERECTED AMID ANTARCTIC WASTES.

It was within a mere eleven miles of One Ton Camp, which would have meant safety to the Antarctic explorers, that the search party found the tent containing the bodies of Captain Scott, Dr E. A. Wilson and Lieutenant H. R. Bowers. This is, perhaps, the most tragic note of the whole Antarctic disaster. Above is the cairn, surmounted with a cross, erected over the tent where the bodies were found. At the side are Captain Scott's skis planted upright in a small pile of frozen snow.

CAPTAIN SCOTT'S DYING APPEAL TO MANHOOD OF BRITAIN.

Last Inspiring Message Found in
Diary of Polar Hero.

'FOR THE HONOUR OF OUR COUNTRY'

Stirring Words of Great Englishman
at Point of Death.

HOW A COMRADE DIED.

For my own sake I do not regret this journey, which has shown that Englishmen can endure hardship, help one another, and meet death with as great fortitude as ever in the past.

(Signed) R. SCOTT
March 25, 1912.

These words from the last 'rough notes' of Robert Falcon Scott, not least of England's heroes, should be emblazoned in letters of gold in every place where Englishmen do congregate.

History records no nobler and more majestic end, no more inspiring death-message than Captain Scott's, the Devonshire sailor who, with his little band of brave men, won to the southernmost goal of modern chivalry and found a continent of ice for their grave and mountains of snow for their tombstone.

The strong man of the party, Petty Officer Evans, was the first to fail. 'He died a natural death, but left us shaken.'

A month later Captain Oates walked out into the blizzard to his death. 'It was the act of a brave man and an English gentleman.'

Three were left. They strove on and camped eleven miles only from their depot, where food and new life awaited them. Eleven miles only after the eternal white walk over 550 miles of snow and ice.

Food gave out and fuel. Death's hand gripped them. 'We are weak, writing is difficult,' scrawled the great leader, but summoned up strength to make an inspiriting appeal, surely the most eloquent ever written, to Britain to 'see that those who are dependent on us are properly provided for.'

Every word in that last tragic message stabs the imagination, every sentence reveals depths of suffering and heroism, the more eloquent for the rugged restraint with which a man of action has set it down.

'This with a sick companion enormously increased our anxieties.' That is all Captain Scott has to say of the unthinkable hardships that must have been caused them by the strong man of the party being converted into a helpless burden, enormously lessening their united resources, insufferably enhancing the weight of their load.

'We knew it was the act of a brave man and an English gentleman.' An English gentleman! What an ideal for the manhood of England. A man walking into the blizzard to his death lest he should be a burden to his fellow-sufferers ...

Immortal as the last words of Sir Philip Sydney and of Nelson should be the last words of Robert Scott, written down in the lingering hours of his death in the Great White Waste.

Captain Oates's self-sacrifice touches our imagination, perhaps, a little more vividly then the resolute patience of his companions. He went forth to meet his fate, knowing well that even the last chance of safety was closed to him. 'The most voluntary death,' said Montaigne, 'is the fairest,' and no one has ever died with a clearer security that death depended upon his own will than Captain Oates.

Rather than be a hindrance to his friends he sought death, the only thing that remained in his power. The time and place invested the deed with a high simplicity. It was no act of violence that he committed. There was not the excitement of the battlefield, with blows given and received. It was enough for him to leave the tent and go out into the blizzard.

'AN ENGLISH GENTLEMAN.'

The few words in which Captain Scott records his death have a poignant eloquence which is beyond the reach of mere literature. They are not likely ever to fall in forgetfulness.

'He slept through the night,' wrote Scott, 'hoping not to wake, but he awoke in the morning. It was blowing a blizzard. Oates said, "I am going outside and I may be some time." He went out into the blizzard and we have not seen him since. We knew that Oates was walking to his death, but though we tried to dissuade him we knew it was the act of a brave man and an English gentleman.'

When he was gone they were able to resume their journey. They resumed it in vain. They died themselves a few days later, a poor eleven miles from safety.

The deaths of Captain Scott and his companions have left for us a legacy, the just pride that their great names are compatriot with our own. They died unfriended and remote, yet without panic, and serenely conscious of the fate which awaited them. Their bravery gives us a confident assurance that the spirit of sacrifice is not extinguished.

HIS DIARY.

Amongst the records found in the tent was Captain Scott's diary. It consisted of ten large volumes written in pencil. It was in perfect condition, after lying for over eight months in that tragic death smitten tent.

The last three volumes were devoted entirely to the dash for the Pole. And there was one remarkable thing to be noted: all through the volumes there was plenty of crossing-out and correcting and rewriting: but the very

last passage – Captain Scott's moving appeal to his country on behalf of the dependants that he and his comrades had left behind them – was written without erasure, interlineation, or correction of any kind.

It is one of the great passages of literature, and even a skilled writer might well have made emendations and corrections before it was in the form that Captain Scott evidently wrote it. As he wrote that wonderful message and appeal just as the end was near, he must have had a great uplifting, a great stirring of the soul.

Captain Scott's final message, written in his diary a little before the end came, is, taken in conjunction with the tragic circumstances, one of the most remarkable pieces of writing in the language.

The death of Captain Scott and his brave companions is already added to the proudest heritage of our race. They are made one with the heroes of all time. Their names are blazoned upon the golden roll of fame.

They have taken their place among the great men who have not hesitated to sacrifice their lives at the bidding of duty, who have followed the lure of an ideal across the trackless paths of an unknown land. The dignity of their death is commensurate with their heroic purpose.

The full, splendid story of all that heroism, self-sacrifice and magnificent devotion to duty in the face of the most terrible sufferings and privations has already been told. It has been told and retold and repeated an hundredfold wherever the English tongue has been spoken. Nothing remains to know of the sad, splendid tragedy. There remained only the photographs recording what had taken place after the gallant five had taken leave of their companions and departed, little pigmy specks, into the Great Unknown about the Pole.

Extract 3.6: *Scott and Amundsen* by Roland Huntford

Huntford's appraisal of Scott and the successful Amundsen created uproar in Britain when it was first published – he was attacking a national hero. In Huntford's account, Scott's party failed because of poor leadership, and Captain Oates' death was the result of pressure from his companions rather than a brave act of self-sacrifice.

At this point one is thrown back on deduction. No medical records have survived, and by now Wilson had stopped keeping his diary. It was in any case intended for his family, and therefore suppressed unpleasantness. He was always sparing of clinical details. His sole explanation of Evans' collapse, for example, was that it had 'much to do with the fact that he has never been sick in his life and is now helpless with his hands frost-bitten', into which worlds can be read. But Wilson was not a practising doctor. His clinical experience was limited, and he showed no evidence of being able to diagnose the complicated progress of scurvy, except in its final stages. And since he was now sick and miserable himself, his desire and capacity to diagnose sickness in others would have been blunted.

What remains are the two records still being kept: Scott's diary, and Bower's meteorological log. From the former comes a tale of dismal pulling and bad surfaces; from the latter, evidence that conditions were not unrelievedly bad, but often the same as those which to Amundsen meant good going. Scott and his companions, however, were so weak that it was clearly an effort to move even their featherweight sledge. They were struggling nine hours or more for their six or seven miles a day.

By now Scott was almost certainly in the early stages of scurvy. He had been out for more than four months without any significant intake of Vitamin C, and his position was complicated by another threat. Stress is a drain on Vitamin C, and of stress Scott and his men had too much. They were beset by fear and anxiety, much of it due to Scott's negligence. He had, for example, not built enough cairns and now, when every minute counted, had to waste time looking for tracks. The sense of being lost is wearing because it strikes at the fundamental human craving for security; nothing can cause panic so easily. Such worries and uncertainty, on top of strains within the party, were enough to waste the life-giving vitamin. Amundsen and his men were spared that drain on their resources.

Oates, Bowers and Wilson were labouring under a terrible burden. Scott alone was still keeping a diary, and his words give a glimpse of what his companions were going through. 'I don't know what I should do,' he wrote on March 4th, 'if Wilson and Bowers weren't so determinedly cheerful over things.' As a leader Scott had collapsed, and Wilson had taken over.

For Oates, it was a *via dolorosa*. He was now unable to pull, just limping along in pain by the side of the sledge, resting when he could. It took him more than an hour to get his swollen feet into his frozen *finnesko* each morning.

One of the effects of scurvy is to make old wounds reopen, because Vitamin C is needed to keep scars together. There are records of injuries opening up again after more than twenty years, as if they had never been healed. Before this stage is reached, there is degeneration in the tissues, which may cause great pain. The lack of Vitamin C from which Oates was now suffering almost certainly affected his old war injury, which was about ten years old. The bullet which smashed his thigh bone had left a massive scar, which by now would have begun to dissolve under incipient scurvy. What he suffered can only be imagined; on top of his frostbitten feet, it merely added to his agony. He was miserable, unnaturally miserable; his old humour dead. He was silent in the tent. As Scott put it in his diary, he had 'become a terrible hindrance'...

Poor Oates. He sat there in the tent, Scott staring at him, with the unspoken expectation of the supreme sacrifice.

At Cape Evans, Oates had emphatically said that on the Polar journey no man should be a burden to his companions. He thought that a pistol should be carried, and 'if anyone breaks down he should have the privilege of using it'.

Perhaps Oates remembered another conversation, a year before, when he told Scott he would regret not taking the ponies on to move One Ton Depot further south, and Scott had replied that he had 'had more than enough of this cruelty to animals, and for the sake of a few marches, I'm not going to defy my feelings'. Scott had saved his feelings, but he had not yet paid the cost.

In the tent that night, Oates turned to Wilson as those in trouble usually did. He had no wish to confide in Scott, for whom by now he had lost any lingering vestige of respect. Oates had to face the hideous realisation that he had been betrayed by incompetent leadership. If only he had not been so mistakenly silent, he could have avoided this futile disaster. It was a heavy burden of regret to bear.

He had left writing until too late, and handed over his fragmentary diary to Wilson, asking him to give it to his mother. She was, he told Wilson, the only woman he had ever loved, and his greatest regret was that he had not written to her now, before the end.

According to Scott's diary, Oates 'slept through the night' – implying that this was no longer usually the case – 'hoping not to wake'. What does this mean? If he could, he would have taken the opium tablets and put himself out of his misery, but that was a moral barrier he could not cross. Probably he appealed to Wilson, and Wilson gave him a morphine injection. It would not have been a fatal dose. For that we have Wilson's word: 'Our record,' as he put it in a letter to his parents, 'is clear.' But he may have given Oates enough to quell his pain, with perhaps the half-admitted thought that in his condition it might be his quietus.

But there was no easy way out for Oates. In the morning he woke. It was, if the dates were right, March 17th, and his thirty-second birthday. The tent walls cracked with the noise of canvas whipped by the wind. He struggled out of the worn, damp furs of his sleeping bag, crawled over his companions' legs across the tent and, taking hold of the entrance, hanging down like an empty sack, he started to undo it. It was the ordinary and familiar act of many a camp. Three pairs of eyes stared; someone made a half-hearted attempt to stop him.

The knot loosened; the sack opened and became a tunnel. Like an animal creeping away to die, Oates limped out into the whirling drift and was seen no more.

Wilson wrote to Mrs Oates that he had never seen or heard of such courage as her son had shown. He died, said Wilson, like a man and a soldier, without a word of complaint.

In Scott's version, as it appeared in his diary, Oates, as he left the tent said: 'I am just going outside and may be some time.' Oates, said Scott,

took pride in thinking that his regiment would be pleased with the bold way in which he met his death… We knew that poor Oates was walking to his death, but… we knew it was the act of a brave man and an English gentleman.

Wilson implies that Oates was suffering so much that, when there was no longer any hope, he took the only way out. Scott ascribes heroic thoughts, leaving the unanswered question of how he knew. Scott, however, was by now writing for publication, some day. Wilson was writing a very personal letter and, if Oates had expressed heroic intent, he would have told Mrs Oates so, including presumably his last words. Where independent testimony exists, Wilson is always reliable.

Scott, however, was preparing his alibi. A subordinate driven to the extremity of suffering would be damaging in the extreme, so Oates simply *had* to have a storybook ending. In any case, Scott, who always went by appearances, may well have interpreted Oates' action as the correct gesture.

The weather lifted and, for a few days more, Scott, Wilson and Bowers struggled on. On March 21st, they came within eleven miles of One Ton Depot, food and fuel almost gone. They pitched their tent and a blizzard came down from the south-west. Scott's right foot had been frostbitten, and he was almost unable to walk. Now he was the drag on the party, and in the predicament of Oates. Wilson and Bowers, in marginally better shape, prepared to set off for the depot and fetch food and fuel. Something stopped them; it is not clear what. Bowers was not the man to give up while there was the ghost of a chance.

Even in top form they had been stopped by the same kind of following gale because of the inability to steer in bad weather. Because of slovenly marking, they needed good weather to find the depot. But the storm is unlikely to have been as fierce or unrelenting as Scott suggested, for even in health he dramatised events. Now he was cold, starving, ill, things might easily seem worse than they were. Scott himself probably held Bowers and Wilson back.

Even if they reached the depot, they were probably finished, with 130 miles still to safety and the season closing in. Scott's frostbitten foot threatened gangrene. 'Amputation is the least I can hope for now,' he wrote, 'but will the trouble spread?' If, by some miracle, they got through, they would probably be crippled for life. All this Wilson, and certainly Bowers, were prepared to accept; but Scott had to face the terrible words MENE MENE TEKEL UPHARSIN... Thou art weighed in the balances and art found wanting.

'I stand or fall by the expedition', Scott had written home before starting. He had nothing to look forward to. He had been beaten to the Pole. He had bungled the whole enterprise. He had departed in triumph, and now he would have to return home and face his public in defeat. At best, what awaited him was the humiliating sympathy reserved for the also-ran. His enemies would laugh at him. Indeed, on March 20th, Armitage, embittered by the *Discovery* expedition, went ashore to send off the press telegram, while *Terra Nova* cruised up and down along the coast to prevent any leakage of news. She entered Lyttelton on February 12th. Flags were at half mast. The headlines streamed across the page. The death of Scott had gripped the world. 'The adventure is finished,' Gran [fellow Scott expedition member] wrote in his diary, 'and our journey lies in the past.'

But all evidence that poor Oates had done away with himself when his pain became too great to bear, especially Wilson's letter to Mrs Oates, was concealed.

Tragedy had to be gilded with heroic gesture, or Scott would have been held responsible, which would not have redounded to his credit.

Nowhere in the records of the Polar party is Oates explicitly said to have given up his life out of heroic self-sacrifice. The tale depends on the hint in Scott's account.

The Oates family were oddly restrained. Mrs Oates had evidently discerned the truth and never forgave Scott. She acted like the mother not of a hero, but of a victim. Nonetheless, she acquiesced in bending her son's behaviour to an acceptable pattern. 'One cannot state facts plainly,' as Teddy Evans wrote to her in all too familiar words, 'when they reflect on the organisation.'

In a typical sermon, preached at the naval dockyard chapel, Devonport, Oates and his companions were praised for 'the reminder they bring us of… the glory of self-sacrifice, the blessing of failure'. A great deal of verbiage was expended on the theme of 'snatching victory from the jaws of death'. Oates was not that kind of person at all; he was far too plain and rational. There was something poignantly symbolic about his action, the aristocrat seeking his end because there was no longer any place for him; it was the only way out.

It was Scott who suited the sermons. His actions and, above all, his literary style, appealed to the spirit of his countrymen. He personified the glorious failure which by now had become a British ideal. He was a suitable hero for a nation in decline.

Few attempts were made to analyse the reasons for disaster. It was less disturbing to make a virtue of calamity and dress up incompetence as heroism. In the face of overwhelming evidence to the contrary, the *Daily Chronicle* wrote that 'Captain Scott's expedition was undoubtedly the best equipped of all those which have explored the Antarctic Continent'. *The Times* offered a typical sophistry. 'Let us put out of our minds all the gossip which... has been circulated about a "race",' it urged – adding that the real value of this Antarctic expedition was

> 'spiritual, and therefore in the truest sense national. It is proof that in an age of depressing materialism men can still be found to face known hardship, heavy risk and even death, in pursuit of an idea... That is the temper of men who build empires, and while it lives among us we shall be capable of maintaining an Empire that our fathers builded.'

Extract 3.7: *Terra Incognita* by Sara Wheeler

Sara Wheeler is a travel writer with a fascination for the Antarctic and its legends. In her writing, you will gain yet another perspective of the story.

It was no longer man against nature, it was man against himself. The diaries reveal a sense of apotheosis: the terrible journey back from the Pole was a moral drama about the attainment of self-knowledge. Scott went to the mountaintop, there on the blanched wasteland. He failed to return from the last journey, but in that failure he found a far more precious success. Defeat on this earthly plane was transfigured. The journey becomes a quest for self-fulfilment, and Scott's triumph is presented as the conquering of the self.

Similarly, after George Mallory and Sandy Irvine disappeared into the mists of Everest twelve years after Scott perished, everyone quickly forgot what had actually happened and glorified the climbers' transcendental achievements. At their memorial service in St Paul's Cathedral, the Bishop of Chester used a quotation from the Psalms to establish a connection between Mallory and Irvine's climb and the spiritual journey upwards, referring to it 'as the ascent by which the kingly spirit goes up to the house of the Lord'. So it was, too, that out of the tent on the polar plateau rose the myth of the saintly hero.

By nimble sleight of hand in their portrayal of Scott, the mythmakers reversed the David and Goliath roles of Norway and Britain. Scott was the gentlemanly amateur who played the game and didn't rely on dogs. Amundsen, on the other hand, was a technological professional who cheated by using dogs. Frank Debenham, Scott's geologist on the *Terra Nova* expedition, wrote in his book *Antarctica: the Story of a Continent*, published in

1959, that both Scott and Shackleton deployed techniques which were slower, more laborious, and failed, but that to criticise them for doing it their way instead of Amundsen's 'is rather like comparing the man who prefers to row a boat across a bay with the man who hoists up a sail to help himself'. Scott's advocates made a virtue of the fact that he had hauled to the Pole without dogs or ponies, and they still do, but this is disingenuous. He had been perfectly prepared to use caterpillar motor-sledges and took three south on the *Terra Nova* (these were a failure). Furthermore, as Debenham himself wrote, 'The fact of the matter is that neither Scott nor Shackleton, the two great exponents of manhauling, understood the management of sledge dogs.'

As he lay dying, Scott somehow found the rhetorical language to invest the whole ghastly business with the currency of nobility. This is his greatest achievement, and with it he paved the way for the making of the legend. 'Had we lived,' he wrote famously, 'I should have had a tale to tell of the hardihood, endurance, and courage of my companions which would have stirred the heart of every Englishman.' He even had the presence of mind to recognise the emotive value of altering 'To My Wife' on Kathleen's envelope to 'To My Widow'. In a few pages he scorched himself into the national consciousness. By the time the letters and diary reached home the spiritual and the national coalesced perfectly. *The Times* said of Scott's last venture, 'The real value of the expedition was spiritual, and therefore in the truest sense national... proof that we are capable of maintaining an Empire.' King George expressed the hope that every British boy could see photographs of the expedition, 'for it will help promote the spirit of adventure that made the empire'. On the wilder shores of journalism Scott actually became the nation: 'Like Captain Scott,' proclaimed

World's Work, 'we are journeying in a cold world towards nothing that we know.' True enough.

Scott touched the imagination of the country and exemplified not just England but a strain of Edwardian manhood. Later, Apsley Cherry-Garrard, who was there, wrote of Scott and his dead men, 'What they did has become part of the history of England, perhaps of the human race, as much as Columbus or the Elizabethans, David, Hector or Ulysses. They are an epic.' In the Great War, Scott became a handy placebo for the soldiers floundering in muddy trenches. Over 100,000 officers and men in France alone saw expedition photographer Herbert Ponting's moving-picture film, and in his book *The Great White South*, Ponting quotes from the following letter despatched by a Forces chaplain ministering to the frontline troops.

> I cannot tell you what a tremendous delight your films are to thousands of our troops. The splendid story of Captain Scott is just the thing to cheer and encourage them out here... The thrilling story of Oates' self-sacrifice, to try and give his friends a chance of 'getting through', is one that appeals to so many at the present time. The intensity of its appeal is realised by the subdued hush and quiet that pervades the massed audience of troops while it is being told. We all feel we have inherited from Oates and his comrades a legacy and heritage of inestimable value in seeing through our present work. We all thank you with very grateful hearts.

When Kathleen Scott died scores of crumpled letters from the front lines were found among her papers, the senders all telling her they could never have faced the dangers and hardships of the war had they not learned to do so from her dead husband's teaching. With Scott, they believed they could rise above it.

Would Scott have become the myth that he is had he lived? I doubt it. The most powerful hero is the dead hero, the one who never loses his teeth. Like Peter Pan, he must never grow old. It is central to the myth of Mallory and Irvine that they died on Everest. Lytton Strachey, who was passionate about Mallory and his Dionysian good looks, perceptively noted before the 1924 expedition even sailed from Birkenhead that the legend of Mallory would only survive if the climber died young. 'If he were to live,' Strachey wrote, 'he'll be an unrecognisable middle-aged mediocrity, probably wearing glasses and a timber toe.' Instead, Mallory became Sir Galahad, like Scott before him.

Though it is tempting to indulge the cliché that a national preference for dead heroes is peculiarly British, an examination of, say, Russian polar literature also reveals a large cast of heroic dead. Like most clichés, however, this one is woven with a thread of truth, and Scott would probably have had to stagger back to the hut to cut much ice with North Americans.

When Tryggve Gran, one of Scott's men, emerged from the tent on the plateau after he had seen the three frozen bodies which had lain there through the long polar night, he said that he envied them. 'They died having done something great,' he wrote. 'How hard death must be having done nothing.'[1]

* * *

---

[1] The importance of Scott's death was brilliantly illustrated in a seven-part Central Television series, *The Last Place on Earth* (screened on PBS in the States), based on Roland Huntford's book. Amundsen, back in Norway after his great triumph, is soaping himself in the bath. His brother and confidant appears in the doorway to tell him that Scott died on the journey back from the Pole. 'So he has won,' says the actor playing Amundsen quietly.

Later, I recognised the gabled ridged roof and weatherboard cladding of the hut in the distance. It was a prefabricated hut, made in England and shipped south in pieces. I once saw a picture of it taken when it was first erected, not at the foot of a smoking Mount Erebus but in a grimy urban street in Poplar in London's East End. The men had stitched quilts with pockets of seaweed to use as insulation between the walls.

When I pushed open the wooden door I smelt my grandmother's house when I was a child – coal dust and burnt coal – and it was chilly, as it used to be at six o'clock in the morning when I followed my grandfather downstairs to scrape out the grate. The Belmont Stearine candles Scott's men had brought were neatly stacked near the door, and the boxes said, 'made expressly for hot climates', which some people would say summed up their preparations. The wrappers bore the picture of a West Indian preparing something delicious on a fire under a palm tree. It was the familiarity of the surroundings which struck my English sensibility – blue-and-orange Huntley and Palmer biscuit boxes, green-and-gold tins of Lyle's golden syrup, blue Cerberos salt tubes and the shape of the label on Heinz tomato ketchup bottles. Atora, Lea and Perrins, Fry's, Rising Sun Yeast ('certain to rise'), Gillards *Real* Turtle Soup – the brand names cemented in our social history. I still lived with many of these products, and the continuum they provided intensified the hut experience. I remembered a very long novel by an American woman called Elizabeth Arthur who had spent some time on the ice. Describing the profoundly moving experience of visiting the hut, she talked about a 'Hunter' and Palmer biscuit box. To an English sensibility this sounds as odd as 'Heinzer' baked beans.

A single beam of sunlight fell on the bunk in Scott's quarters, the small space immortalised by Ponting and described by Teddy Evans as the 'Holy of Holies'. On the desk, someone – a good artist – had drawn a tiny bird in violet ink on the crisp ivory page of a pocket notebook. Unlike Shackleton, Scott separated the quarters of men and officers, and the difference is often deployed to illustrate their contrasting styles of leadership. Wayland Young, Baron Kennet of the Dene and Kathleen Scott's son by her second marriage, has set out a convincing defence of Scott's decision. As far as the state of class divisions in the Navy was concerned, Young wrote that it was 'unchanged for 1,000 years, so to complain about it now is no more interesting or original than to complain about it in the army of Wellington, Marlborough, Henry V or Alfred the Great'.

They were extremely resourceful. Clissold, the cook, rigged up a device whereby a small metal disc was placed on top of rising dough, and when it reached the right height it came into contact with another piece of metal, and an electrical circuit rang a bell next to his bunk. The battered books included Kipling (of course), and a tiny edition of *The Merry Wives of Windsor* held together with string, in the fly of which a spidery hand had inscribed Milton's 'When will the ship be here/Come sing to me.' There is something disingenuous about Scott's hut, however, just as there is about the myth. The mummified penguin lying open-beaked and akimbo next to a copy of the *Illustrated London News* had been placed there by the New Zealand Antarctic Heritage people, and Ponting's photographs show that Scott's desk is not the original (the replacement was brought over from the Cape Royds hut). The historic huts were often plundered in the early days. Richard Pape visited Cape Evans in 1959 with one of the American Operation Deep Freezes under Admiral Dufek. In his very bad book, *Poles Apart*, he records quite candidly that he pocketed 'a glass inkwell on which

"R. F. Scott" had been painted, also a bottle of Indian ink marked "Wilson"'.

Still, I saw them everywhere. A gap in a row of cuphooks, the dented rubber of a Wellington boot tossed aside, a carefully re-rolled bandage, the whiff of Ponting's developing fluid in his tiny darkroom, a half-spent candle in a chipped candlestick – perhaps it was the whistling of the wind, but I swear I could have turned round and seen them tramping back, spent dogs at their heels.

Later, the public manipulated the myth according to its own needs and ends. A crackpot society called the Alliance of Honour, founded in 1903 and devoted to purity, had spawned flourishing branches in 67 countries by the 1930s. The Alliance was vigorously opposed to masturbation, and the following quotation is culled from its voluminous literature: 'We may safely assert that among the heroes of that dreadful journey from the South Pole there were no victims of the vice which the Alliance seeks to combat.'

Secondhand bookshops are rife with musty first editions of the diaries inscribed in a Sunday School teacher's best copperplate, rewarding a child for good attendance. I found a 1941 bus ticket pressed inside one of them. It was a tough time to be living in London, and perhaps the diaries helped. During the Second World War the calls of the legend were legion, and they were often voiced by cranks. In 1941 Kathleen received a letter from a woman in New York who said she had borne Scott's illegitimate child when she was fifteen. A handwritten note on the envelope said, 'The lady is now dead.'

A few years after the war crocodiles of schoolchildren marched through provincial towns and into cavernous cinemas to watch *Scott of the Antarctic*. John Mills had already played countless war heroes, so he was a prepacked role model. By the mid-fifties, however, liberals at least were suspicious of the myth and had lost faith in the concept of England. In Peter Vansittart's recent book of social and cultural commentary, *In the Fifties*, he recalls a game he devised during that period to test the objectivity of his intellectual chums. He would read out a passage from Scott's diaries, including 'We are showing that Englishmen can still die with a bold spirit, fighting it out to the end…' Assuming that Vansittart was being ironic, the audience tittered. Later he amended the reading to make it sound as if it had come from the Warsaw Ghetto in 1944, or from Mao Tsetung, and on those occasions his friends applauded respectfully.

Shibboleths were mocked. Scott became a cliché. In the Monty Python television sketch 'Scott of the Sahara', the captain fights a 25-foot electric penguin. Similarly, Scott appears as an astronaut in Tom Stoppard's play *Jumpers*, written in 1972. The first Englishman to reach the moon, Scott's triumph is overshadowed by the plight of his only colleague Astronaut Oates. Scott kicks Oates to the ground at the foot of the spacecraft ladder and pulls it in behind him with the words, 'I am going up now, I may be some time.'

Historical revisionism is as unavoidable as the grave: it pursues leading figures of any age long after their work on earth is done. In the 1970s, when imperialism was widely reviled, Roland Huntford published his joint biography *Scott and Amundsen* (called *The Last Place on Earth* in the States), a passionate book which sought to demolish the Scott myth, suggesting not only that Scott was mortal, but that he was an unpleasant character and a poor leader. According to Huntford, he used science only as an excuse to participate in the race, unlike Amundsen 'who did not stoop to use science as an agent of prestige'. Nobody had criticised Scott before, and Huntford did so comprehensively. Many felt inclined to agree with him, while the keepers of the flame would have had him sent to the Tower. The book whipped up a blizzard of angry protests, vitriolic reviews and a furious exchange of correspondence and 'statements' in national newspapers, including lengthy debate provoked by Huntford's assertion that Kathleen Scott had sex with Nansen while her husband was slogging up a glacier and was worried about becoming pregnant. The central argument was over how she recorded the arrival of her periods in her diary. How disappointing it had to come to that.

Wayland Young wrote an article refuting Huntford's criticism of Scott for *Encounter* magazine in May 1980. He demonstrates the weakness of portions of Huntford's scholarship. Others had pressed Huntford on the same points raised by Young, and in October 1979 the biographer was obliged to admit on national television that his description of Scott staring at Oates in the tent at the end to try to force him to his death was based on *intuition*. In short, he got carried away by his own argument. Prejudice is not necessarily fatal in a biography, however, and Huntford's book is intelligent, gripping, full of insight and elegantly written. I enjoyed it as much as any polar book I have read, and a good deal more than most of them. It is a pity that Huntford was quite so obsessed with the destruction of the legend, for if he had reined in his prejudices he could have produced a masterpiece.

A similar controversy raged in the Norwegian press after a book was published portraying Amundsen as a bounder and Scott a man worthy of beatification. Kåre Holt's *The Race*, published in English in 1974, was admittedly a novel; it was nonetheless a useful counterweight to Huntford's book. Bob Headland, archivist at the Scott Polar Research Institute, told me that he likes to keep the two volumes next to one another on the shelf, 'preferably with a layer of asbestos between them'.

'The Scandinavians', Huntford told me when I met him at Wolfson College in Cambridge for lunch in a dining hall smelling of boiled cauliflower, 'by and large set out from a country at ease with itself. They have no need for an ego boost. They are not play-acting. The Norwegian will always look for a glimpse of the sun, because he actually wants to be happy'. Self-delusion, he said, was the besetting sin of the British. 'Scott and Amundsen inhabited totally different mental worlds,' he added, leaning across the table conspiratorially. 'You mustn't be deluded by the fact that they were contemporaries. The Scandinavians live in a landscape which has enormous natural power, so that when they go to the polar regions it's sort of an extension of what they are.'

Huntford lived in Scandinavia for many years ('mainly because I like skiing'). He writes exceptionally well about polar scenery; so well that it is hard to imagine him not hankering to go south himself. When I put this to him, he prevaricated.

'No,' he said eventually. 'These are landscapes of the mind, you see.'

He had referred obliquely to a note written by Bowers on the back of one of Wilson's last letters; it apparently indicated that Bowers died last, but Huntford said the envelope had been suppressed by the people at Scott Polar Research Institute in order to maintain Scott's preeminence. When I asked them, they denied it. Who cares? I wanted to know about the power of the human spirit to transcend mortality, and what one human heart can learn from another, not whose aorta packed up first.

Extract 3.8: 'In From the Cold...', *The Observer Review*

This piece was written as a review of Susan Solomon's book, *The Coldest March: Scott's Fatal Antarctic Expedition*. It shows how historical events continue to be interpreted in new ways.

17 BOOKS
The Observer Review 7 October 2001

In from the cold ...

Scott of the Antarctic was beaten by the weather – not ineptitude

ROBERT MACFARLANE

The Coldest March: Scott's Fatal Antarctic Expedition
by Susan Solomon
Yale University Press £19.95, pp383

Stories of polar exploration are clearly answering a powerful cultural need at present. Susan Solomon's *The Coldest March* is highly original, beautifully presented and remarkably modest. The book is the fruit of Solomon's long-standing professional involvement with Antarctica and its history (she is an American atmospheric scientist specialising in Antarctica). Her thesis is simple and controversial: that Scott and his team, who froze to death only a few miles from safety, died not because of ineptitude – the popular legend of the bumbling Brits – but due to freakishly cold temperatures. 'One has a horrible feeling that this is a real bad season,' Scott had noted ominously in his diary before the final march began. By comparing the team's scrupulous temperature readings from 1911–12, with years of meteorological data gathered from the weather stations which now mark Scott's 'via dolorosa', Solomon proves Scott's prescience.

The case for Scott as a delinquent leader is on the face of it persuasive. His gaffes have been well-publicized – the ponies he took were ill-chosen; his men contracted scurvy because they didn't eat enough seal meat; he took five men to the pole instead of four; they lugged back 35lb of rock from a geologizing side-trip when they should have been thinking about survival. The list goes on. Crucial to the case for the prosecution, too, is the contrast between Amundsen – the sleek Scandinavian, strong of thigh, quick of mind and ineffably efficient – and Scott: a cross between fuddled First World War brigadier and an over-impetuous schoolboy, full of earnestness but fatally lacking in common-sense.

What Solomon convincingly argues, though, is that none of

Scott's alleged blunders was serious enough to cause the death of the party. In her book, what undoubtedly killed Scott and his team was the extreme cold they faced on their return march from the Pole, when the temperature fell as low as -42°C; far below the seasonal average. This cold turned the men's clothing into suits of armour and their sleeping bags into scabbards of ice, and it caused all of them (Scott in particular) to suffer grievously from frostbite.

However – and this is the clinching point of Solomon's brilliant argument – it wasn't just extra discomfort which the team had to cope with. Each man was hauling a sledge weighing about 200lb, and sledges work on a principle of lubrication: the movement of the sled's runners creates friction, which melts the ice crystals they are moving over, thus supplying a vital lubricating layer of liquid between runner and ice. When the temperature falls below a certain point, however, the ice is no longer melted by the friction and the sled's runners no longer run.

So on the way back from the Pole, Scott and his men suddenly found themselves dragging 200lb dead weights. Unsurprisingly, they were unable to make the headway they had expected: the unseasonable cold stopped them dead in their tracks.

There is now a permanent South Pole Station, where scientists clink glasses and drink to Scott in the thermostat-controlled warmth all year round. Modernity has tamed even the Antarctic, that least tractable of lands. But the stories of its exploration have gained in power. Scott and his men did not possess what Hemingway called 'grace under pressure' – the elegant insouciance in the face of danger which was for him exemplified by the matador – but what they did display was almost inconceivable resilience to personal suffering, combined with an attentiveness to the beauty of the landscape they moved in. These qualities, plus the intense pathos of their failure, are what moves us about them, and Susan Solomon is as alert to the emotional implications of Scott's story as she is to the meteorological ones. She has written a marvellous and complex book at once a detective story, a brilliant vindication of a maligned man, and an elegy both for Scott and his men, and for the 'crystalline continent' on which they died.

Activities

'Guidance for Visitors', Atlas Travel and The Lonely Planet – Antarctica

These extracts are written for people considering visiting the Antarctic, so have a shared *audience*. However, there are differences in the *purpose*. You are going to explore the ways in which the differing purposes are evident through content, style and language.

1   Complete the chart below with examples from the texts. Do this in groups and share your results.

	'Guidance for Visitors'	Atlas Travel	The Lonely Planet
Persuades • Use of poetic/ informal/dramatic language • Use of illustrations			
Informs • Detailed information • Organisation of information • Range of information included, e.g. historic, scientific, tourist events			
Instructs • Use of imperative • Use of formal language			
Describes • Focus on attractions – how described			

• Focus on dangers – how described			
I think the purpose of this piece of writing is . . .			

a You can check your findings against a grid describing the features of different types of non-fiction writing – ask your teacher for a copy.

Captain Scott's Diary – The Last March

1 Read through the diary extracts and the message to the public.

   a What picture of the sufferings and subsequent death of Captain Oates are we given?

   b How did Captain Scott and the other men seem to regard Oates?

   c What impression did Captain Scott wish to leave of himself and his fellow explorers?

2 You could analyse this through creating a bank of impressions under these headings:

   • descriptions of Oates
   • descriptions of bravery/dedication
   • descriptions of private despair/loss of hope
   • descriptions of putting on a brave face/keeping up morale.

3 Look again at the message to the public, and the ways in which Scott explains and justifies. Make a note of:

   • use of phrases implying a factual, objective account
   • how Scott introduces new paragraphs and organises information.

   What impression does he create of the reasons for failure?

4   After reading these extracts, can you understand why Captain Scott and his companions became national heroes?

'Captain Scott's Tomb', *The Daily Mirror*

1   Read the *Daily Mirror* newspaper article of 1913. Create a list of shared adjectives describing the men's actions and their sufferings. Which adjectives are used by both Scott and the newspaper? What does this suggest about Scott's intentions in his writing?

2   Collect examples of dramatic language from the newspaper, e.g. *Death's hands gripped them; stabs the imagination; immortal last words*. What responses is the writer trying to create in the readers?

3   What reasons for the disaster are given? Is Scott's analysis questioned?

4   This story was written in 1913, before the outbreak of the First World War.

   a What picture of British qualities is the writer trying to create?

   b What evidence of extreme patriotism can you find?

   c Why might these sort of attitudes be important in a country when it embarks on a major war?

Scott and Amundsen

1   Read through Huntford's account. Compare his description of the men and their behaviour with Scott's. Then look for:

   a evidence for Huntford's opinions in Scott's account, e.g. Scott appearing to blame Oates for Wilson's exhaustion

   b Huntford's use of tentative expressions, e.g. *may have*; *almost certainly*; *perhaps* – what does this indicate?

2   Compare Huntford's depiction of life in the tent with Scott's. Try to find examples of contrasting language.

How does each describe:

- the condition of the men and how they are coping
- their attitudes to each other
- the death of Oates.

3   What actual evidence does Huntford have? Where is he using evidence, and where is he relying on conjecture? How does he use language to create the impressions he wants?

Terra Incognita

1   Read the extract, then in a group or pair, discuss these questions.

   a   How does this change your view of Huntford's work?

   b   Consider the following statements, then discuss how these might affect the way you read works of history.

   - Historical revisionism[1] is as unavoidable as the grave
   - Prejudice is not necessarily fatal in a biography.

2   Does Wheeler think historical/factual accuracy is important? What does she look for in a book? Do you agree with her priorities?

3   How does Wheeler account for the hero worship that has grown up around Scott? How does this differ from Huntford's view? Can you find evidence for either in Scott's writings and the contemporary news article?

'In From the Cold', *The Observer Review*

1   Read this article carefully. How does it affect your view of i) events and ii) historians? Discuss your thoughts about this as a group.

2   How do the language, layout and viewpoint differ from the 1913 article in the *Daily Mirror* (page 79)? Make a list of these differences.

---

1 Historical revisionism means looking again at evidence and interpreting it in a new way, often to challenge an established or accepted view.

Section 4
Handle With Caution

People say that life is the thing, but I prefer reading.
Logan Pearsall Smith, 1865–1946

Never sign a valentine with your own name.
Charles Dickens, *The Pickwick Papers* 1812–1870

The extracts in this section explore the effects of reading
– sometimes positive, sometimes dangerous.

Extract 4.1: From 'Bernice Bobs Her Hair' by F. Scott Fitzgerald

'Bernice Bobs Her Hair' was Fitzgerald's fourth story for the *Saturday Evening Post* (1 May 1920). It occupies an important position in the Fitzgerald catalogue as a witty early treatment of a characteristic subject that he would later examine more seriously: the competition for social success and the determination with which his characters – especially the young women – engage in it. The story was based on a detailed memo Fitzgerald wrote to his younger sister, Annabel, advising her how to achieve popularity with boys.

No matter how beautiful or brilliant a girl may be, the reputation of not being frequently cut in on[1] makes her position at a dance unfortunate. Perhaps boys prefer her company to that of the butterflies with whom they dance a dozen times an evening, but youth in this jazz-nourished generation is temperamentally restless, and the idea of fox-trotting more than one full fox trot with the same girl is distasteful, not to say odious. When it comes to several dances and the intermissions between she can be quite sure that a young man, once relieved, will never tread on her wayward toes again.

Warren danced the next full dance with Bernice, and finally, thankful for the intermission, he led her to a table on the veranda. There was a moment's silence while she did unimpressive things with her fan.

---

1 'cut in on': when a boy and girl were dancing, it was customary for another boy to 'cut in' and take the girl for his partner. The original boy could not leave his partner until this happened. To be 'cut in on' often was a sign of popularity.

'It's hotter here than in Eau Claire,' she said.

Warren stifled a sigh and nodded. It might be for all he knew or cared. He wondered idly whether she was a poor conversationalist because she got no attention or got no attention because she was a poor conversationalist.

'You going to be here much longer?' he asked, and then turned rather red. She might suspect his reasons for asking.

'Another week,' she answered, and stared at him as if to lunge at his next remark when it left his lips.

Warren fidgeted. Then with a sudden charitable impulse he decided to try part of his line on her. He turned and looked at her eyes.

'You've got an awfully kissable mouth,' he began quietly.

This was a remark that he sometimes made to girls at college proms when they were talking in just such half dark as this. Bernice distinctly jumped. She turned an ungraceful red and became clumsy with her fan. No one had ever made such a remark to her before.

'Fresh!'[2] – the word had slipped out before she realised it, and she bit her lip. Too late she decided to be amused, and offered him a flustered smile.

Warren was annoyed. Though not accustomed to have that remark taken seriously, still it usually provoked a laugh or a paragraph of sentimental banter. And he hated to be called fresh, except in a joking way. His charitable impulse died and he switched the topic.

'Jim Strain and Ethel Demorest sitting out as usual,' he commented.

This was more in Bernice's line, but a faint regret mingled with her relief as the subject changed. Men did not talk to her about kissable mouths, but she knew that they talked in some such way to other girls.

---

2 'fresh': bold, cheeky, taking flirting a bit too far.

'Oh, yes,' she said, and laughed. 'I hear they've been mooning round for years without a red penny. Isn't it silly?'

Warren's disgust increased. Jim Strain was a close friend of his brother's, and anyway he considered it bad form to sneer at people for not having money. But Bernice had had no intention of sneering. She was merely nervous.

II

When Marjorie and Bernice reached home at half after midnight they said good night at the top of the stairs. Though cousins, they were not intimates. As a matter of fact Marjorie had no female intimates – she considered girls stupid. Bernice on the contrary all through this parent-arranged visit had rather longed to exchange those confidences flavoured with giggles and tears that she considered an indispensable factor in all feminine intercourse. But in this respect she found Marjorie rather cold; felt somehow the same difficulty in talking to her that she had in talking to men. Marjorie never giggled, was never frightened, seldom embarrassed, and in fact had very few of the qualities which Bernice considered appropriately and blessedly feminine.

As Bernice busied herself with toothbrush and paste this night she wondered for the hundredth time why she never had any attention when she was away from home. That her family were the wealthiest in Eau Claire; that her mother entertained tremendously, gave little dinners for her daughter before all dances and bought her a car of her own to drive round in, never occurred to her as factors in her home-town social success. Like most girls she had been brought up on the warm milk prepared by Annie Fellows Johnston and on novels in which the female was beloved because of certain mysterious womanly qualities, always mentioned but never displayed.

Bernice felt a vague pain that she was not at present engaged in being popular. She did not know that had it not been for Marjorie's campaigning she would have danced the entire evening with one man; but she knew that even in Eau Claire other girls with less position and less pulchritude were given a much bigger rush. She attributed this to something subtly unscrupulous in those girls. It had never worried her, and if it had her mother would have assured her that the other girls cheapened themselves and that men really respected girls like Bernice.

She turned out the light in her bathroom, and on an impulse decided to go in and chat for a moment with her aunt Josephine, whose light was still on. Her soft slippers bore her noiselessly down the carpeted hall, but hearing voices inside she stopped near the partly opened door. Then she caught her own name, and without any definite intention of eavesdropping lingered – and the thread of the conversation going on inside pierced her consciousness sharply as if it had been drawn through with a needle.

'She's absolutely hopeless!' It was Marjorie's voice. 'Oh, I know what you're going to say! So many people have told you how pretty and sweet she is, and how she can cook! What of it! She has a bum time. Men don't like her.'

'What's a little cheap popularity?'

Mrs Harvey sounded annoyed.

'It's everything when you're eighteen,' said Marjorie emphatically. 'I've done my best. I've been polite and I've made men dance with her, but they just won't stand being bored. When I think of that gorgeous colouring wasted on such a ninny, and think what Martha Carey could do with it – oh!'

'There's no courtesy these days.'

Mrs Harvey's voice implied that modern situations were too much for her. When she was a girl all young ladies who belonged to nice families had glorious times.

'Well,' said Marjorie, 'no girl can permanently bolster up a lame-duck visitor, because these days it's every girl for herself. I've even tried to drop her hints about clothes and things, and she's been furious – given me the funniest looks. She's sensitive enough to know she's not getting away with much, but I'll bet she consoles herself by thinking that she's very virtuous and that I'm too gay and fickle and will come to a bad end. All unpopular girls think that way.'

Marjorie considered whether or not convincing her mother was worth the trouble. People over forty can seldom be permanently convinced of anything. At eighteen our convictions are hills from which we look; at forty-five they are caves in which we hide.

Having decided this, Marjorie said good-night. When she came out into the hall it was quite empty.

III

While Marjorie was breakfasting late next day Bernice came into the room with a rather formal good morning, sat down opposite, stared intently over and slightly moistened her lips.

'What's on your mind?' inquired Marjorie, rather puzzled.

Bernice paused before she threw her hand-grenade.

'I heard what you said about me to your mother last night.'

Marjorie was startled, but she showed only a faintly heightened colour and her voice was quite even when she spoke.

'Where were you?'

'In the hall. I didn't mean to listen – at first.'

After an involuntary look of contempt Marjorie

dropped her eyes and became very interested in balancing a stray cornflake on her finger.

'I guess I'd better go back to Eau Claire – if I'm such a nuisance.' Bernice's lower lip was trembling violently and she continued on a wavering note: 'I've tried to be nice, and – and I've been first neglected and then insulted. No one ever visited me and got such treatment.'

Marjorie was silent.

'But I'm in the way, I see. I'm a drag on you. Your friends don't like me.' She paused, and then remembered another one of her grievances. 'Of course I was furious last week when you tried to hint to me that that dress was unbecoming. Don't you think I know how to dress myself?'

'No,' murmured Marjorie less than half-aloud.

'What?'

'I didn't hint anything,' said Marjorie succinctly. 'I said, as I remember, that it was better to wear a becoming dress three times straight than to alternate it with two frights.'

'Do you think that was a very nice thing to say?'

'I wasn't trying to be nice.' Then after a pause: 'When do you want to go?'

Bernice drew in her breath sharply.

'Oh!' It was a little half-cry.

Marjorie looked up in surprise.

'Didn't you say you were going?'

'Yes, but –'

'Oh, you were only bluffing!'

They stared at each other across the breakfast-table for a moment. Misty waves were passing before Bernice's eyes, while Marjorie's face wore that rather hard expression that she used when slightly intoxicated undergraduates were making love to her.

'So you were bluffing,' she repeated as if it were what she might have expected.

Bernice admitted it by bursting into tears. Marjorie's eyes showed boredom.

'You're my cousin,' sobbed Bernice. 'I'm v-v-visiting you. I was to stay a month, and if I go home my mother will know and she'll wah-wonder –'

Marjorie waited until the shower of broken words collapsed into little sniffles.

'I'll give you my month's allowance,' she said coldly, 'and you can spend this last week anywhere you want. There's a very nice hotel –'

Bernice's sobs rose to a flute note, and rising of a sudden she fled from the room.

An hour later, while Marjorie was in the library absorbed in composing one of those non-committal, marvellously elusive letters that only a young girl can write, Bernice reappeared, very red-eyed and consciously calm. She cast no glance at Marjorie but took a book at random from the shelf and sat down as if to read. Marjorie seemed absorbed in her letter and continued writing. When the clock showed noon Bernice closed her book with a snap.

'I suppose I'd better get my railroad ticket.'

This was not the beginning of the speech she had rehearsed upstairs, but as Marjorie was not getting her cues – wasn't urging her to be reasonable; it's all a mistake – it was the best opening she could muster.

'Just wait till I finish this letter,' said Marjorie without looking round. 'I want to get it off in the next mail.'

After another minute, during which her pen scratched busily, she turned round and relaxed with an air of 'at your service.' Again Bernice had to speak.

'Do you want me to go home?'

'Well,' said Marjorie, considering, 'I suppose if you're not having a good time you'd better go. No use being miserable.'

'Don't you think common kindness – '

'Oh, please don't quote "Little Women"!' cried Marjorie impatiently. 'That's out of style.'

'You think so?'

'Heavens, yes! What modern girl could live like those inane females?'

'They were the models for our mothers.'

Marjorie laughed.

'Yes, they were – not! Besides, our mothers were all very well in their way, but they know very little about their daughters' problems.'

Bernice drew herself up.

'Please don't talk about my mother.'

Marjorie laughed.

'I don't think I mentioned her.'

Bernice felt that she was being led away from her subject.

'Do you think you've treated me very well?'

'I've done my best. You're rather hard material to work with.'

The lids of Bernice's eyes reddened.

'I think you're hard and selfish, and you haven't a feminine quality in you.'

'Oh, my Lord!' cried Marjorie in desperation. 'You little nut! Girls like you are responsible for all the tiresome colourless marriages; all those ghastly inefficiencies that pass as feminine qualities. What a blow it must be when a man with imagination marries the beautiful bundle of clothes that he's been building ideals round, and finds that she's just a weak, whining, cowardly mass of affectations!'

Bernice's mouth had slipped half open.

'The womanly woman!' continued Marjorie. 'Her whole early life is occupied in whining criticisms of girls like me who really do have a good time.'

Bernice's jaw descended farther as Marjorie's voice rose.

'There's some excuse for an ugly girl whining. If I'd been irretrievably ugly I'd never have forgiven my parents for bringing me into the world. But you're starting life without any handicap' – Marjorie's little fist clinched. 'If you expect me to weep with you you'll be disappointed. Go or stay, just as you like.' And picking up her letters she left the room.

Bernice claimed a headache and failed to appear at luncheon. They had a matinée date for the afternoon, but the headache persisting, Marjorie made explanation to a not very downcast boy. But when she returned late in the afternoon she found Bernice with a strangely set face waiting for her in her bedroom.

'I've decided,' began Bernice without preliminaries, 'that maybe you're right about things – possibly not. But if you'll tell me why your friends aren't – aren't interested in me I'll see if I can do what you want me to.'

Marjorie was at the mirror shaking down her hair.

'Do you mean it?'

'Yes.'

'Without reservations? Will you do exactly what I say?'

'Well, I –'

'Well nothing! Will you do exactly as I say?'

'If they're sensible things.'

'They're not! You're no case for sensible things.'

'Are you going to make – to recommend –'

'Yes, everything. If I tell you to take boxing-lessons you'll have to do it. Write home and tell your mother you're going to stay another two weeks.'

Extract 4.2: *The Princess Bride* by William Goldman

William Goldman explains how the unexpected discovery of a great book transformed his attitude to reading as a teenager.

This is my favourite book in all the world, though I have never read it.

How is such a thing possible? I'll do my best to explain. As a child, I simply had no interest in books. I hated reading, I was very bad at it, and besides, how could you take the time to read when there were games that shrieked for playing? Basketball, baseball, marbles – I could never get enough. I wasn't even good at them, but give me a football and an empty playground and I could invent last-second triumphs that would bring tears to your eyes. School was torture. Miss Roginski, who was my teacher for the third through fifth grades, would have meeting after meeting with my mother. 'I don't feel Billy is perhaps extending himself quite as much as he might.' Or, 'When we test him, Billy does really exceptionally well, considering his class standing.' Or, most often, 'I don't know, Mrs Goldman: what *are* we going to do about Billy?'

What *are* we going to do about Billy? That was the phrase that haunted me those first ten years. I pretended not to care, but secretly I was petrified. Everyone and everything was passing me by. I might have admitted that, for all my frenzy, I was very much alone.

'What *are* we going to do about you, Billy?'

'I don't know, Miss Roginski.'

'How could you have failed this reading test? I've heard you use every word with my own ears.'

'I'm sorry, Miss Roginski. I must not have been thinking.'

'You are always thinking, Billy. You just weren't thinking about the reading test.'

I could only nod.

She sagged at her desk. 'You've got a wonderful imagination, Billy.'

I don't know what I said. Probably 'thank you' or something.

'I can't harness it, though,' she went on. 'Why is that?'

'I think it's that probably I need glasses and I don't read because the words are so fuzzy. That would explain why I'm all the time squinting. Maybe if I went to an eye doctor who could give me glasses I'd be the best reader in class and you wouldn't have to keep me after school so much.'

She just pointed behind her. 'Get to work cleaning the blackboards, Billy.'

'Yes, ma'am.' I was the best at cleaning blackboards.

'Do they look fuzzy?' Miss Roginski said after a while.

'Oh, no, I just made that up.' I never squinted either. But she just seemed so whipped about it. She always did. This had been going on for three grades now.

'I'm just not getting through to you somehow.'

'It's not your fault, Miss Roginski.'

'You're going to be all right, Billy.'

'I sure hope so, Miss Roginski.'

'You're a late bloomer, that's all. Winston Churchill was a late bloomer and so are you.'

I was about to ask her who he played for but there was something in her tone that made me know enough not to.

'And Einstein.'

Him I also didn't know. Or what a late bloomer was either. But boy, did I ever want to be one.

* * *

When I was twenty-six, my first novel, *The Temple of Gold*, was published by Alfred A. Knopf. Before publication, the publicity people at Knopf were talking to me, trying to figure what they could do to justify their salaries, and they asked who did I want to send advance copies to that might be an opinion maker, and I said I didn't know anybody like that and they said, 'Think, everybody knows somebody,' and I got all excited because the idea just came to me and I said, 'Okay, send a copy to Miss Roginski,' which I figure was logical and terrific because if anybody made my opinions, she did. (She's all through *The Temple of Gold*, by the way, only I called her 'Miss Patulski' – even then I was creative.)

'Send it to Highland Park Grammar School,' I said, and first what I thought I'd write was 'For Miss Roginski, a rose from your late bloomer,' but then I thought that was too conceited, so I decided 'For Miss Roginski, a weed from your late bloomer,' would be more humble. Too humble, I decided next, and that was it for bright ideas that day. I couldn't think of anything. Then I thought, What if she doesn't even remember me? Hundreds of students over the years, why should she? So finally in desperation I put, 'For Miss Roginski from William Goldman – Billy you called me and you said I would be a late bloomer and this book is for you and I hope you like it. I was in your class for third, fourth and fifth grades, thank you very much. William Goldman.'

The book came out and got bombed; I stayed in and did the same; adjusting. Not only did it establish me as the freshest thing since Kit Marlowe, it also didn't get read by anybody. Not true. It got read by a number of people, all of whom I knew. I think it is safe to say, however, no strangers savoured it. It was a grinding experience and I reacted as indicated above. So when

Miss Roginski's note came – late – it got sent to Knopf and they took their time relaying it – I was ready for a lift.

'Dear Mr. Goldman: Thank you for the book. I have not had time yet to read it, but I am sure it is a fine endeavour. Of course I remember you. I remember all my students. Yours sincerely, Antonia Roginski.'

What a crusher. She didn't remember me at all. I sat there holding the note, rocked. People don't remember me. Really. It's not any paranoid thing; I just have this habit of slipping through memories. It doesn't bother me all that much, except I guess that's a lie; it does. For some reason, I test very high on forgettability.

So when Miss Roginski sent me that note making her just like everyone else, I was glad she'd never gotten married. I'd never liked her anyway, she'd always been a rotten teacher, and it served her right her first name was Antonia.

'I didn't mean it,' I said out loud right then. I was alone in my one-room job on Manhattan's glamorous West Side and talking to myself. 'I'm sorry, I'm sorry,' I went on. 'You've got to believe that, Miss Roginski.'

What had happened, of course, was that I'd finally seen the postscript. It was on the back of the thank-you note and what it said was, 'Idiot. Not even the immortal S. Morgenstern could feel more parental than I.'

S. Morgenstern! *The Princess Bride*. She remembered!
Flashback.
1941. Autumn.

Pneumonia today is not what it once was, especially when I had it. Ten days or so in the hospital and then home for the long recuperating period. I guess it was three more weeks in bed, a month maybe. No energy, no games even. I just was this lump going through a strength-gathering time, period.

Which is how you have to think of me when I came upon *The Princess Bride*.

It was my first night home. Drained; still one sick cookie. My father came in, I thought to say good night. He sat on the end of my bed. 'Chapter One. The Bride,' he said.

It was then only I kind of looked up and saw he was holding a book. That alone was surprising. My father was next to illiterate. In English. He came from Florin (the setting of *The Princess Bride*) and there he had been no fool. He said once he would have ended up a lawyer, and maybe so.

Anyway, I said, 'Huh? What? I didn't hear.' I was so weak, so terribly tired.

'Chapter One. The Bride.' He held up the book then. 'I'm reading it to you for relax.' He practically shoved the book in my face. 'By S. Morgenstern. Great Florinese writer. *The Princess Bride*. He too came to America. S. Morgenstern. Dead now in New York. The English is his own. He spoke eight tongues.'

'Has it got any sports in it?'

'Fencing. Fighting. Torture. Poison. True love. Hate. Revenge. Giants. Hunters. Bad men. Good men. Beautifulest ladies. Snakes. Spiders. Beasts of all natures and descriptions. Pain. Death. Brave men. Coward men. Strongest men. Chases. Escapes. Lies. Truths. Passion. Miracles.'

'Sounds okay,' I said, and I kind of closed my eyes. 'I'll do my best to stay awake... but I'm awfully sleepy, Daddy...'

Who can know when this world is going to change? Who can tell before it happens, that every prior experience, all the years, were a preparation for... nothing. Picture this now, an all-but-illiterate old man struggling with an enemy tongue, an all-but-exhausted young boy fighting against sleep. And nothing between them but the words of another alien, painfully translated from native sounds to foreign. Who could suspect that in the morning a different child would wake? I remember, for myself, only trying to beat back fatigue. Even a week later I was not aware of what had begun that night, the doors that were slamming shut while others slid into the clear. Perhaps I should have at least known something, but maybe not; who can sense revelation in the wind?

What happened was just this: I got hooked on the story.

For the first time in my life, I became actively interested in a *book*. Me the sports fanatic, me the game freak, me the only ten-year-old in Illinois with a hate on for the alphabet wanted to know *what happened next*.

What became of beautiful Buttercup and poor Westley and Inigo, the greatest swordsman in the history of the world? And how really strong was Fezzik and were there limits to the cruelty of Vizzini, the devil Sicilian?

Each night my father read to me, chapter by chapter, always fighting to sound the words properly, to nail down the sense. And I lay there, eyes kind of closed, my body slowly beginning the long flow back to strength. It took, as I said, probably a month, and in that time he read *The Princess Bride* twice to me. Even when I was able to read myself, this book remained his. I would never have dreamed of opening it. I wanted his voice, his sounds. Later, years later even, sometimes I might say, 'How about the duel on the cliff with Inigo and the man in black?' and my father would gruff and grumble and get the book and lick his thumb, turning pages till the mighty battle began. I loved that. Even today, that's how I summon back my father when the need arises. Slumped and squinting and halting over words, giving me Morgenstern's masterpiece as best he could. *The Princess Bride* belonged to my father.

Everything else was mine.

There wasn't an adventure story anywhere that was safe from me. 'Come on,' I would say to Miss Roginski when I was well again. 'Stevenson, you keep saying Stevenson, I've finished Stevenson, who now?' and she would say, 'Well, try Scott, see how you like him,' so I tried old Sir Walter and I liked him well enough to butt through a half-dozen books in December (a lot of that was Christmas vacation when I didn't have to interrupt my reading for anything but now and then a little food). 'Who else, who else?' 'Cooper maybe,' she'd say, so off I went into *The Deerslayer* and all the Leatherstocking stuff, and then on my own one day I stumbled onto Dumas and D'Artagnan and that got me through most of February, those guys. 'You have become, before my very eyes, a novel-holic,' Miss Roginski said. 'Do you realise you are spending more time now reading than you used to spend on games? Do you know that your arithmetic grades are actually getting worse?' I never minded when she knocked me. We were alone in the schoolroom, and I was after her for something good to devour. She shook her head. 'You're certainly blooming, Billy. Before my very eyes. I just don't know into what.'

I just stood there and waited for her to tell me to read somebody.

'You're impossible, standing there waiting.' She thought a second. 'All right, try Hugo. *The Hunchback of Notre Dame.*'

'Hugo,' I said. '*Hunchback*. Thank you,' and I turned, ready to begin my sprint to the library. I heard her words sighed behind me as I moved.

'This can't last. It just can't last.'

But it did.

Extract 4.3: 'It's A Boy Thing' by Lyn Gardner

This article is concerned with the trend for teenage boys to stop reading, and is written to advise parents

IT'S A BOY
THING

Male teens will happily devour a football fanzine but will balk at the idea of looking at a novel. It's time to make reading cool again, says Lyn Gardner

Dave is 15 and a Manchester United fan. He says that he hasn't read a novel for pleasure since primary school. Dave is bright enough, with good grades in nine GCSEs. It is not that he can't read but that, like many teenage boys, he won't read. At least not fiction. He has devoured the biographies and autobiographies of everybody connected with Man U, regularly reads football magazines and is just getting into the kind of magazines aimed at the young men's market. But novels, forget it. Reading just isn't cool.

Dave is pretty typical of male teenagers. The reading trends that are apparent in primary school come to fruition in the teenage years. By the age of six, girls are already reading more than boys, and by the teenage years the gap has widened. In a sample conducted by Exeter University in 1998, only 18% of 14- and 15-year-old boys had read a book for pleasure the previous evening. Seven years previously of similar survey found that 25% of boys had read for pleasure the previous night.

Should we be worried? Yes and no. There is clear evidence that wide-ranging reading has a positive impact on educational attainment in all areas and that it can be an enormously pleasurable experience. Reading, particularly novels, can offer adolescents a glimpse into other worlds and other experiences that in real life they might never come across. Great books such as Robert Cormier's and Melvin Burgess's novels provide vivid emotional insights and landscapes that the average male adolescent might ignore or reject in real life. Reading offers an emotional dimension to teenage male lives and allows them to reflect on thoughts and feelings that they might find it difficult to discuss with parents and find not cool to discuss with friends.

But reading for pleasure assumes that you have plenty of leisure time. Many argue that it is the rise of the computer and the internet that is deflecting teenage attention from books. But while there is evidence that increasing numbers of teenagers prefer to research homework from the net rather than from the printed page, there is little to suggest that technology is edging out reading. It is just that like modern adults, adolescents have a wider choice of leisure pursuits coupled with far less leisure time.

Take Alasdair, a bright 17-year-old just about to enter his second sixth-form year at an Oxford comprehensive. Alasdair is a keen reader but even he was taken aback when in the summer before entering the sixth form he was given a reading list comprising some 70 classic novels that it was felt that students should have read before embarking on the A-level English course. He now says that his course work requires so much reading and reading around the subject that he has far less time than he would like to read for pleasure.

There is, of course, a world of difference between the book you

have to read and the book that you choose to read, and it would be a pity if government bids to raise literacy standards and exam pass rates actually end up turning boys away from books rather than firing their enthusiasm.

So what can be done? The first and obvious things is to catch them when they are young. Boys who don't read for pleasure in primary school are unlikely to be transformed into enthusiastic readers in their teens. Reading is a habit that you pick up. If you live in a household where adults seldom read and there are no books, you are unlikely to pick up the habit.

Many parents make the mistake of stopping reading to their children as soon as children get to the stage when they can decode the squiggles for themselves. By the ages of 9 or 10 very few parents regularly read with and to their children. But sharing books is great fun and helps to develop the reading habit that lasts a lifetime.

Don't get too het up about what it is that they are reading. If it is that biography of Pele or an R. L. Stine chiller that takes their fancy, don't try and push Charles Dickens down their throats. School may too often treat books as if they are medicine, but teenage boys will only read if they perceive reading as being as much fun as playing Tomb Raider.

Extract 4.4: 'The Defense of Poesy' by Sir Philip Sidney

Here Sir Philip Sidney is arguing for 'poesy', which in his day meant stirring classical tales dealing with gods, heroes, battles and monsters. Many of his arguments could still be used today to describe the pleasures and effects of reading.

And first, truly, to all them that, professing learning, inveigh against poetry, may justly be objected that they go very near to ungratefulness, to seek to deface that which, in the noblest nations and languages that are known, hath been the first light-giver to ignorance, and first nurse, whose milk by little and little enabled them to feed afterwards of tougher knowledges.

Only the poet, disdaining to be tied to any such subjection, lifted up with the vigor of his own invention, doth grow, in effect, into another nature, in making things either better than nature bringeth forth, or, quite anew, forms such as never were in nature, as the heroes, demi-gods, cyclops, chimeras, furies, and such like; so as he goeth hand in hand with nature, not enclosed within the narrow warrant of her gifts, but freely ranging within the zodiac of his own wit. Nature never set forth the earth in so rich tapestry as divers poets have done; neither with pleasant rivers, fruitful trees, sweet-smelling flowers, nor whatsoever else may make the too-much-loved earth more lovely; her world is brazen, the poets only deliver a golden.

Poesy, therefore, is an art of imitation, for so Aristotle termeth it in his word [Greek], that is to say, a representing, counterfeiting, or figuring forth; to speak metaphorically, a speaking picture, with this end, – to teach and delight.

Now therein of all sciences – I speak still of human, and according to the human conceit – is our poet the monarch. For he doth not only show the way, but giveth so sweet a prospect into the way as will entice any man to enter into it. Nay, he doth, as if your journey should lie through a fair vineyard, at the very first give you a cluster of grapes, that full of that taste you may long to pass further. He beginneth not with obscure definitions, which must blur the margent with interpretations, and load the memory with doubtfulness. But he cometh to you with words set in delightful proportion, either accompanied with, or prepared for, the well-enchanting skill of music; and with a tale, forsooth, he cometh unto you, with a tale which holdeth children from play, and old men from the chimney-corner, and, pretending no more, doth intend the winning of the mind from wickedness to virtue; even as the child is often brought to take most wholesome things, by hiding them in such other as to have a pleasant taste, – which, if one should begin to tell them the nature of the aloes or rhubarb they should receive, would sooner take their physic at their ears than at their mouth. So is it in men, most of which are childish in the best things, till they be cradled in their graves, – glad they will be to hear the tales of Hercules, Achilles, Cyrus, Æneas; and, hearing them, must needs hear the right description of wisdom, valour and justice; which, if they had been barely, that is to say philosophically, set out, they would swear they be brought to school again.

Activities

'Bernice Bobs Her Hair'

This story was written in 1920, a time when young women were abandoning the Victorian ideals with which their mothers were brought up and becoming more recognisably 'modern'.

1 First impressions of Bernice. Read parts I and II and answer the following questions.

   a Bernice is shy with boys and doesn't really know how to talk to them. This might have been ideal modesty in Victorian times but means she is regarded as a bore. How does Fitzgerald describe her actions/reactions? Note his use of adjectives and adverbs.

   b Why do you think Fitzgerald uses Warren's narrative viewpoint at this stage in the story? What is he showing us about the effect Bernice has on boys?

2 Bernice and Marjorie:

   a How do the cousins differ?

   b What expectations does Bernice have of friendship? How does Marjorie disappoint these?

3 Bernice and books:

   a What books influenced Bernice's ideas as she was growing up?

   b Why do you think Fitzgerald describes these as 'warm milk'? (Think about who warm milk is usually fed to, and what this implies about the way women used to be regarded.)

4 Now read Part III. Look at the conversations between Bernice and Marjorie. How far do you agree with these descriptors of both?

Bernice: weak; manipulative; vulnerable; emotional; blackmailing; victim; self-pitying; dishonest; plays games.

Marjorie: honest; bullying; direct; strong; cold; practical; unkind; doesn't play games; controlling.

Whether you agree or disagree, try to support your opinion with evidence from the text.

5 How does Fitzgerald use the novel *Little Women* as a focus for their differences? What does each of the girls think of the book?

6 'a weak, whining, cowardly mass of affectations'. How far can this description be applied to Bernice?

7 Which character emerges as the most attractive? What do you think Fitzgerald wanted us to think of each?

8 Look at the end of the extract. Try to predict what you think might happen next in the story. Get hold of a copy of it and see if your predictions are right.

The Princess Bride

1 Compare the verbs and adjectives associated with reading and those associated with games. What impression is created?

2 'What *are* we going to do about Billy?' What does this suggest about the importance adults attach to reading? Why do you think this is?

3 His father tries to draw him in with 'Fencing. Fighting. Torture. Poison.'. What does this suggest about boys' interests?

4 Why do you think the boy became interested in the story? Give reasons.

5 The boy says: 'Come on' and 'Who else? Who else?' What does this tell us about his attitude to reading at the end?

6 Compare the verbs and adjectives used about reading at the end of the extract to those at the beginning. What has the writer done?

'It's a Boy Thing'

1 This article is concerned with the trend for teenage boys to stop reading, and is written to advise parents. The author uses specific devices to make her writing sound convincing. Find examples of:

a rhetorical questions which she answers herself

b examples/anecdotes from her own experience to support ideas.

2 When you have identified some examples, discuss why they help to make an argument convincing.

3 Because this piece is written for a particular purpose/audience, there are some marked features of style. Identify some examples of these and try to link them to purpose/audience:

- use of slang/use of more formal language
- addresses the reader in the second person (you)
- use of the imperative (instruction form)
- generalisations to support argument
- use of first person observation only to support argument
- definite statements
- tentative statements.

4 For discussion: Consider this article along with *The Princess Bride* extract. Do you agree that there is a problem with encouraging boys to read? Do girls and boys read differently? Are you a keen male reader?

5 Activities:

a In a group, create booklists for readers of your age that would appeal to boys or girls, or both.

b Write an article for teachers (you could try to get it published in one of the professional magazines) advising them on ways to enthuse readers of either gender.

'The Defense of Poesy'

1 Structure: Create a summary of Sir Philip Sidney's argument in flow-chart form.

  a In each box summarise the main point.

  b Then create a series of bullet points listing his supporting statements in brief.

  c Now create a plan for an argument of your own justifying reading for a modern audience, following Sidney's overall line, but updating language and examples.

2 The effects of reading:

  a How does Sidney describe the beneficial effects of reading? List his main points.

  b Now look at at least two other extracts from this section that seem to make similar points – you could do this in a group and create a chart for a range of the extracts.

3 Similes: Find examples of Sidney using simile to convey the effect of poetry.

  a Discuss why you think he has chosen these.

  b Create some similes of your own to describe the effect a good writer has on a reader.

  c Look at the likening of hiding a moral in the tale to giving children medicine hidden in something sweet – can you think of any modern examples from the media of this technique?

4 Language:

a Look at the ways in which Sidney introduces new paragraphs and moves the argument on. Which connectives are still commonly used?

b Look at his way of presenting ideas within clauses – compare this with the Francis Bacon extract, *Of Parents and Children* (page 40).

5 Researching references/further reading: Sidney refers to **Hercules**, **Achilles**, **Cyrus** and **Aeneas**. Find out about these stories and who wrote them. What elements live on today and how?

Section 5

The Sincerest Form of Flattery: Parody and Satire

Parodies and caricatures are the most penetrating of criticisms.

Aldous Huxley, 1894–1963

Satire should, like a polished razor keen,
Wound with a touch that's scarcely felt or seen.

Lady Mary Wortley Montague, 1689–1762

The extracts in this section consist of some literary parodies, and the original texts on which they are based.

Satire has been described as seeking to expose folly or vice, with a view to correction. The pieces in this section are selected to show examples of satire which target big corporations.

Writers of parodies use some of the same techniques as cartoonists – they take distinguishing features of their subject, and exaggerate them to an extreme point. Other parodies simply rely on our familiarity with the original, and present it to us in a different form. Much parody relies on the fact that it treats literature humorously, when we are used to seeing it taken very seriously. Parodies can also highlight how attitudes have changed over time. They enable us to laugh at the concerns of our forebears with a comfortable sense of our superiority.

Extract 5.1: *Jane Eyre* by Charlotte Brontë

Jane Eyre is a young governess who has just started
work at the mysterious Thornfield Hall, where strange
noises and laughter can be heard from the attic floor
bedrooms. Although she is small, poor and plain, Jane
has the courage to stand up for herself during her first
meeting with her enigmatic new boss, Mr Rochester.

Two wax candles stood lighted on the table, and two on
the mantelpiece; basking in the light and heat of a superb
fire, lay Pilot – Adèle knelt near him. Half reclined on a
couch appeared Mr Rochester, his foot supported by a
cushion; he was looking at Adèle and the dog. The fire
shone full on his face. I knew my traveller, with his broad
and jetty eyebrows, his square forehead, made squarer by
the horizontal sweep of his black hair. I recognised his
decisive nose, more remarkable for character than
beauty; his full nostrils, denoting, I thought, choler; his
grim mouth, chin, and jaw – yes, all three were very grim,
and no mistake. His shape, now divested of cloak, I
perceived harmonised in squareness with his
physiognomy. I suppose it was a good figure in the
athletic sense of the term – broad-chested and thin-
flanked, though neither tall nor graceful.

Mr Rochester must have been aware of the entrance of
Mrs Fairfax and myself; but it appeared he was not in the
mood to notice us, for he never lifted his head as we
approached.

'Here is Miss Eyre, sir,' said Mrs Fairfax, in her quiet
way. He bowed, still not taking his eyes from the group of
the dog and child.

'Let Miss Eyre be seated,' said he: and there was
something in the forced stiff bow, in the impatient yet
formal tone, which seemed further to express, 'What the

deuce is it to me whether Miss Eyre be there or not? At this moment I am not disposed to accost her.'

I sat down quite disembarrassed. A reception of finished politeness would probably have confused me: I could not have returned or repaid it by answering grace and elegance on my part; but harsh caprice laid me under no obligation; on the contrary, a decent quiescence, under the freak of manner, gave me the advantage. Besides, the eccentricity of the proceedings was piquant: I felt interested to see how he would go on.

He went on as a statue would, that is, he neither spoke nor moved. Mrs Fairfax seemed to think it necessary that someone should be amiable, and she began to talk. Kindly, as usual – and, as usual, rather trite – she condoled with him on the pressure of business he had had all day; on the annoyance it must have been to him with that painful sprain: then she commended his patience and perseverance in going through with it.

'Madam, I should like some tea,' was the sole rejoinder she got. She hastened to ring the bell; and when the tray came, she proceeded to arrange the cups, spoons, etc., with assiduous celerity. I and Adèle went to the table; but the master did not leave his couch.

'Will you hand Mr Rochester's cup?' said Mrs Fairfax to me; 'Adèle might perhaps spill it.'

I did as requested. As he took the cup from my hand, Adèle thinking the moment propitious for making a request in my favour, cried out:

'N'est-ce pas, monsieur, qu'il y a un cadeau pour Mademoiselle Eyre dans votre petit coffre?'

'Who talks of cadeaux?' said he gruffly. 'Did you expect a present, Miss Eyre? Are you fond of presents?' And he searched my face with eyes that I saw were dark, irate and piercing.

'I hardly know, sir; I have little experience of them: they are generally thought pleasant things.'

'Generally thought? But what do *you* think?'

'I should be obliged to take time, sir, before I could give you an answer worthy of your acceptance: a present has many faces to it, has it not? And one should consider all, before pronouncing an opinion as to its nature.'

'Miss Eyre, you are not so unsophisticated as Adèle: she demands a "cadeau", clamorously, the moment she sees me: you beat about the bush.'

'Because I have less confidence in my deserts than Adèle has: she can prefer the claim of old acquaintance, and the right too of custom; for she says you have always been in the habit of giving her playthings; but if I had to make out a case I should be puzzled, since I am a stranger, and have done nothing to entitle me to an acknowledgement.'

'Oh, don't fall back on over-modesty! I have examined Adèle, and find you have taken great pains with her: she is not bright, she has no talents; yet in a short time she has made much improvement.'

'Sir, you have now given me my "cadeau"; I am obliged to you: it is the meed teachers most covet – praise of their pupils' progress.'

'Humph!' said Mr Rochester, and he took his tea in silence.

Extract 5.2: 'Miss Mix' by Bret Harte

This extract parodies the first meeting between Jane Eyre and Mr Rochester by exaggerating the language, setting and characters of the original piece.

Chapter II

Blunderbore Hall, the seat of James Rawjester, Esq., was encompassed by dark pines and funereal hemlocks on all sides. The wind sang weirdly in the turrets and moaned through the long-drawn avenues of the park. As I approached the house I saw several mysterious figures flit before the windows, and a yell of demoniac laughter answered my summons at the bell. While I strove to repress my gloomy forebodings, the housekeeper, a timid, scared-looking old woman, showed me into the library.

I entered, overcome with conflicting emotions. I was dressed in a narrow gown of dark serge, trimmed with black bugles. A thick green shawl was pinned across my breast. My hands were encased with black half-mittens worked with steel beads; on my feet were large patterns, originally the property of my deceased grandmother. I carried a blue cotton umbrella. As I passed before a mirror, I could not help glancing at it, nor could I disguise from myself the fact that I was not handsome.

Drawing a chair into a recess, I sat down with folded hands, calmly awaiting the arrival of my master. Once or twice a fearful yell rang through the house, or the rattling of chains, and curses uttered in a deep, manly voice, broke upon the oppressive stillness. I began to feel my soul rising with the emergency of the moment.

'You look alarmed, miss. You don't hear anything, my dear, do you?' asked the housekeeper nervously.

'Nothing whatever,' I remarked calmly, as a terrific scream, followed by the dragging of chairs and tables in the room above, drowned for a moment my reply. 'It is the silence, on the contrary, which has made me foolishly nervous.'

The housekeeper looked at me approvingly, and instantly made some tea for me.

I drank seven cups; as I was beginning the eighth, I heard a crash, and the next moment a man leaped into the room through the broken window.

Chapter III

The crash started me from my self-control. The housekeeper bent toward me and whispered:

'Don't be excited. It's Mr Rawjester – he prefers to come in sometimes in this way. It's his playfulness, ha! ha! ha!'

'I perceive,' I said calmly. 'It's the unfettered impulse of a lofty soul breaking the tyrannising bonds of custom.' And I turned toward him.

He had never once looked at me. He stood with his back to the fire, which set off the Herculean breadth of his shoulders. His face was dark and expressive; his underjaw squarely formed, and remarkably heavy. I was struck with his remarkable likeness to a Gorilla.

As he absently tied the poker into hard knots with his nervous fingers, I watched him with some interest. Suddenly he turned toward me:

'Do you think I'm handsome, young woman?'

'Not classically beautiful,' I returned calmly; 'but you have, if I may so express myself, an abstract manliness, a sincere and wholesome barbarity which, involving as it does the naturalness—' but I stopped, for he yawned at that moment – an action which singularly developed the immense breadth of his lower jaw – and I saw he had forgotten me. Presently he turned to the housekeeper:

'Leave us.'

The old woman withdrew with a courtesy.

Mr Rawjester deliberately turned his back upon me and remained silent for twenty minutes. I drew my shawl the more closely around my shoulders and closed my eyes.

'You are the governess?' at length he said.

'I am, sir.'

'A creature who teaches geography, arithmetic, and the use of the globes – ha! – a wretched remnant of femininity, a skimp pattern of girlhood with a premature flavour of tea-leaves and morality. Ugh!'

I bowed my head silently.

'Listen to me, girl!' he said sternly; 'this child you have come to teach – my ward – is not legitimate. She is the offspring of my mistress, a common harlot. Ah! Miss Mix, what do you think of me now?

'I admire,' I replied, calmly, 'your sincerity. A mawkish regard for delicacy might have kept this disclosure to yourself. I only recognise in your frankness that perfect community of thought and sentiment which should exist between original natures.'

I looked up; he had already forgotten my presence, and was engaged in pulling off his boots and coat. This done, he sank down in an armchair before the fire, and ran the poker wearily through his hair. I could not help pitying him.

The wind howled dismally without, and the rain beat furiously against the windows. I crept toward him and seated myself on a low stool beside his chair.

Presently he turned, without seeing me, and placed his foot absently in my lap. I affected not to notice it. But he started and looked down.

'You here yet, Carrothead? Ah, I forgot. Do you speak French?'

'*Oui, Monsieur.*'

'*Taisez-vous!*' he said sharply, with a singular purity of accent. I complied. The wind moaned fearfully in the chimney, and the light burned dim. I shuddered in spite of myself. 'Ah, you tremble, girl!'

'It is a fearful night.'

'Fearful! Call you this fearful, ha! ha! ha! Look! You wretched little atom, look!' And he dashed forward, and, leaping out of the window, stood like a statue in the pelting storm, with folded arms. He did not stay long, but in a few minutes returned by way of the hall chimney. I saw from the way that he wiped his feet on my dress that he had again forgotten my presence.

'You are a governess. What can you teach?' he asked, suddenly and fiercely thrusting his face in mine.

'Manners!' I replied calmly.

'Ha! Teach *me*!'

'You mistake yourself,' I said adjusting my mittens. 'Your manners require not the artificial restraint of society. You are radically polite; this impetuosity and ferociousness is simply the sincerity which is the basis of a proper deportment. Your instincts are moral; your better nature, I see, is religious. As St Paul justly remarks – see chap. 6, 8, 9 and 10—'

He seized a heavy candlestick, and threw it at me. I dodged it submissively, but firmly.

'Excuse me,' he remarked, as his under-jaw slowly relaxed. 'Excuse me, Miss Mix – but I can't stand St Paul! Enough – you are engaged.'

Extract 5.3: 'The Pig on Ted Hughes' by Bill Greenwell

This poem parodies Ted Hughes' famous poem 'View of a pig'. Before reading the parody, look at the original poem in the 'Authors and Their Craft' section on page 200. Consider Hughes' advice on writing poetry in the accompanying extract from *Learning to Think*. How well does the parody follow Hughes' recommendations?

The man stood with his biro poised.
He was paid, they said, as much as three men.
His jutting jaw, thick furrowed eyebrows.
These jotters stand right out.

His gait and native Yorkshire grit
Seemed to me a bloody cheek.
I was just a dead porker, not yet sliced.
And he wanted his pound of flesh.

He clocked me one with his fist.
It did not seem to bother him,
Smacking my crackling. His kind
Are always coining it with animals.

Even bacon deserves a bit of respect.
That includes bluff, gruff Northern sorts.
This git in the old leather jacket,
How would he like to be soused in hot water?

Extract 5.4: *Pride and Porringers* by E.O. Parrott

In this parody, the language and attitudes found in Jane Austen's novels are grafted onto a familiar story. See Section 1 'You Just Don't Understand' for the original – *Pride and Prejudice*.

Elizabeth laid aside her diary. Her recollection of the scene was sharper than the few inadequate sentences which she had penned the same evening.

'See, Mr Bear,' her mother had said, surveying the dining-room, 'there have been callers in our absence, and not a servant to receive them, and we all out walking. I cannot think why, since I abominate the pursuit, especially in woods. They are so tedious. The quantity of trees makes for considerable monotony.'

'It must be the new tenants of Polar Hall,' she went on, with growing apprehension. 'The shame of it, when I have begged and prayed to you, Mr Bear, to call there, for at least a week.'

Mr Bear observed that it had seemed to him a much longer period.

'Mr Bruin, a wealthy young man with an independent income from stocks, and a very plain sister, so Lady Grizzly informs me.'

Mrs Bear did not say whether the sister was regarded as an enhancement or as an impediment to the aforementioned fortune.

'For I am sure,' she went on, 'that all our old neighbours would know our "at home" days.'

'Mama, one bowl of porridge has been quite eaten up!'

'And so I should have presumed, Elizabeth, for I am sure I make very good porridge, quite the nicest to be found in any of the better houses in these parts – unlike Lady Grizzly's, which has always such obtrusive lumps.

Yes, it must have been the Bruins who called, so mortifying when our neighbourhood so lacks eligible bachelors for Lizzie.'

'I am sure, Mama,' said Elizabeth gravely, 'I could not regard a man as a prospective husband until I had met him and found him to be agreeable in ways unconnected with his fortune.'

'What an obstinate, talkative minx you are becoming, Miss!' exclaimed Mrs Bear with some annoyance.

'Perhaps you should withdraw to your room, Lizzie,' said her father. 'This may not be the moment for such opinions.'

He was regarding the wreckage of a small chair. 'It would appear,' he went on, after Elizabeth had left the room, 'that gentility does not necessarily go hand-in-hand with gentleness in the matter of furniture, at least.'

'I daresay the Bruins are accustomed to such superior chairs that they found our old ones insufficient for them. I am positively ashamed of...'

Her disenchantment with her household belongings was interrupted by a loud cry and a scrambling sound.

'That was Lizzie's voice,' said Mr Bear. 'But, look!'

He drew his spouse's attention to a fair-haired girl who, at that moment, dropped lightly upon the lawn and rapidly retreated into the concealing shelter of the trees.

'So it was not the Bruins who partook of our comestibles, Mrs Bear.'

'I am sure that it was not your fault that it wasn't,' said Mrs Bear. 'Now, you must call on them before such an incident as we have imagined does occur. Mr Bruin might suit Lizzie very well. I cannot think what has happened to the girl, I am sure. She has become such a chatterbox. Though, of course, marriage may cure her, or not, as the case may be.'

Mr Bear observed that to his certain knowledge, entering into wedlock had very little or no effect upon such matters.

Extract 5.5: BADvertising and Adbusters

The material here comes from an American
organisation, BADvertising and a Canadian-based
foundation, Adbusters. They are concerned about the
effects of corporate advertising and the focus here is
the selling of image to young people. They also give
detailed instructions on how to create your own
alternative advertising campaign.

You've come a long way, baby

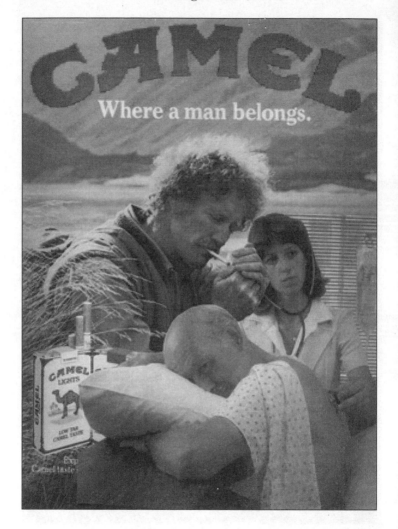

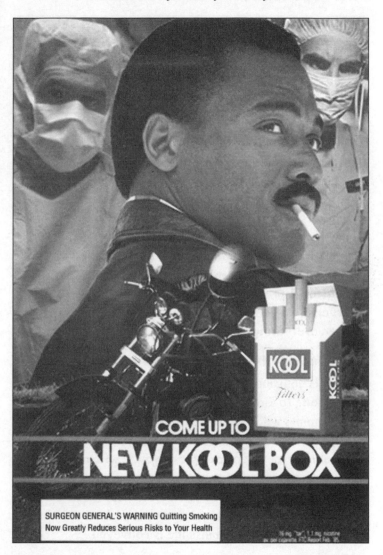

HOW TO CREATE YOUR OWN PRINT AD

1 Decide on your communication objective

The communication objective is the essence of your message. If you want to tell people not to eat turnips because they are picked by migrant workers who are treated cruelly, then that's your communication objective. A word of caution: though perhaps the most important of your 8 steps, this is also the one that beginners tend most to neglect. A precise and well-defined objective is crucial to a good ad. If your objective isn't right on, then everything that follows will be off as well.

2 Decide on your target audience

Who is your message intended for? If you're speaking to kids, then your language and arguments will have to be understandable to kids. On the other hand, if you're speaking to high income earners (for exmple, if you're writing an ad to dissuade people from wearing fur coats), then your language will have to be more sophisticated. So define who your target audience is, because that will decide how your message is conveyed.

3 Decide on your format

Is it going to be a poster, a half-page magazine ad or

a tiny box in the corner of a newspaper? Make this decision based on the target audience you're trying to reach and the amount of money you can afford to spend. If you're talking to kids, a poster in one high school will not only cost less, it will actually reach more of your target audience than a full-page ad in the biggest paper in town. When it comes to deciding on the size of your ad, the more expensive it will be to produce and run. Don't let that discourage you. You can do a lot with a small ad so long as it's strong, clear and properly targeted.

4 Develop your concept

The concept is the underlying creative idea that drives your message. Even in a big ad campaign, the concept will typically remain the same from one ad to another and from one medium to another. Only the execution of that concept will change. So by developing a concept that is effective and powerful, you open the door to a number of very compelling ads. So take your time developing a concept that's strong.

Typically, an ad is made up of a photograph or a drawing (the 'visual'), a headline and writing (the 'copy'). Whether you think of your visual or your headline first makes little difference. However, this diagram shows a few guidelines worth following:

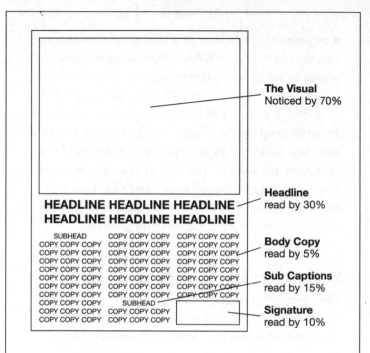

The Visual
Noticed by 70%

Headline
read by 30%

Body Copy
read by 5%

Sub Captions
read by 15%

Signature
read by 10%

5 The visual

Though you don't absolutely require a visual, it will help draw attention to your ad. Research indicates that 70% of people will only look at the visual in an ad, whereas only 30% will read the headline. So if you use a visual, then you're already talking to twice as many people as you otherwise might. Another suggestion is to use photographs instead of illustrations whenever possible. People tend to relate to realistic photographs more easily than unrealistic ones. But whether you choose a photograph or an illustration, the most important criteria is that image be the most interesting one possible and at least half your ad whenever possible.

6 The headline

The most important thing to remember here is that your headline must be short and snappy and must touch the people that read it. Your headline must affect the reader emotionally, either by making them laugh, making them angry, making them curious or making them think. If you can't think of a headline that does one of these four things, then keep thinking. Here's a little tip that might help: try to find an insight or inner truth to the message that you're trying to convey, something that readers will easily relate to and be touched by. Taking the turnips example once again, it might be tempting to write a headline like; 'Stop Exploiting These Migrant Workers.' However, with a little thought, a more underlying truth might be revealed – that Migrant Workers are as human as we are and that our actions do hurt them. From that inner truth, you might arrive at the headline: 'Do unto others as you would have them do unto you'. Of course, the headline doesn't have to be biblical, though that in itself will add meaning and power for many people. Finally, whenever possible, avoid a headline longer than fifteen words. People just don't read as much as they used to.

7 The copy

Here's where you make the case. If you have compelling arguments, make them. If you have persuasive facts, state them. But don't overwhelm with information. Two strong arguments will make more of an impression than a dozen weaker ones. Finally, be clear, be precise and be honest. Any hint of deception will instantly detract from your entire message. Position your copy beneath the headline, laid out in two blocks two or three inches in length. Only about 5% of people will read your copy, whereas 30% will read your headline. By positioning your copy near your heading, you create a visual continuity which will draw more people to the information you want to convey. Use a serif typeface for your copy whenever possible. Those little lines and swiggles on the letters make the reading easier and more pleasing to the eye.

Subheads
If you have lots of copy, break it up with interesting subheads, as we've done in the diagram above. This will make your ad more inviting, more organised and easier to read.

The signature
This is where the name of the organisation belongs, along with the address and phone number. If you don't have an organisation, then

think of a name that will help reinforce the message you're trying to convey. Perhaps 'Citizens for Fairness to Migrant Turnip Pickers' would work for the example we've been using. This isn't dishonest. Your organisation doesn't have to be incorporated or registered for it to be real.

8 Some mistakes to avoid

The single most common mistake is visual clutter. Less is always better than more. So if you're not certain whether something is worth including, then leave it out. If your ad is chaotic, people will simply turn the page and your message will never be read. The second most common mistake is to have an ad that's unclear or not easily understood (haven't you ever looked at an ad and wondered what it was for?). The best way to safeguard against this is to do some rough sketches of your visual with the headline and show it around. If people aren't clear about your message, then it's probably because your message is unclear. And however tempting, don't argue with them or assume that they're wrong and that your ad is fine. You'll be in for an unpleasant surprise. Proofread your ad, then give it to others to proofread, then proofread it yet again. Typographical errors diminish your credibility and have an uncanny habit of creeping into ads when you least expect it.

Extract 5.6: 'Filboid Studge, The Story of a Mouse that Helped' by Saki (H.H. Munro)

This short story both satirises big business and advertising, and subverts the conventions of fairy tales.

'I want to marry your daughter,' said Mark Spayley with faltering eagerness. 'I am only an artist with an income of two hundred a year, and she is the daughter of an enormously wealthy man, so I suppose you will think my offer a piece of presumption.'

Duncan Dullamy, the great company inflator, showed no outward sign of displeasure. As a matter of fact, he was secretly relieved at the prospect of finding even a two-hundred-a-year husband for his daughter Leonore. A crisis was rapidly rushing upon him, from which he knew he would emerge with neither money nor credit; all his recent ventures had fallen flat, and flattest of all had gone the wonderful new breakfast food, Pipenta, on the advertisement of which he had sunk such huge sums. It could scarcely be called a drug in the market; people bought drugs, but no one bought Pipenta.

'Would you marry Leonore if she were a poor man's daughter?' asked the man of phantom wealth.

'Yes,' said Mark, wisely avoiding the error of over-protestation. And to his astonishment Leonore's father not only gave his consent, but suggested a fairly early date for the wedding.

'I wish I could show my gratitude in some way,' said Mark with genuine emotion. 'I'm afraid it's rather like the mouse proposing to help the lion.'

'Get people to buy that beastly muck,' said Dullamy, nodding savagely at a poster of the despised Pipenta, 'and you'll have done more than any of my agents have been able to accomplish.'

'It wants a better name,' said Mark reflectively, 'and something distinctive in the poster line. Anyway, I'll have a shot at it.'

Three weeks later the world was advised of the coming of a new breakfast food, heralded under the resounding name of 'Filboid Studge'. Spayley put forth no pictures of massive babies springing up with fungus-like rapidity under its forcing influence, or of representatives of the leading nations of the world scrambling with fatuous eagerness for its possession. One huge sombre poster depicted the Damned in Hell suffering a new torment from their inability to get at the Filboid Studge which elegant young fiends held in transparent bowls just beyond their reach. The scene was rendered even more gruesome by a subtle suggestion of the features of leading men and women of the day in the portrayal of the Lost Souls; prominent individuals of both political parties. Society hostesses, well-known dramatic authors and novelists, and distinguished aeroplanists were dimly recognisable in that doomed throng; noted lights of the musical-comedy stage flickered wanly in the shades of the Inferno, smiling still from force of habit, but with the fearsome smiling rage of baffled effort. The poster bore no fulsome allusions to the merits of the new breakfast food, but a single grim statement ran in bold letters along its base: 'They cannot buy it now.'

Spayley had grasped the fact that people will do things from a sense of duty which they would never attempt as a pleasure. There are thousands of respectable middle-class men who, if you found them unexpectedly in a Turkish bath, would explain in all sincerity that a doctor had ordered them to take Turkish baths; if you told them in return that you went there because you liked it, they would stare in pained wonder at the frivolity of your motive. In the same way, whenever a massacre of

Armenians is reported from Asia Minor, everyone assumes that it has been carried out 'under orders' from somewhere or another, no one seems to think that there are people who might *like* to kill their neighbours now and then.

And so it was with the new breakfast food. No one would have eaten Filboid Studge as a pleasure, but the grim austerity of its advertisement drove housewives in shoals to the grocers' shops to clamour for an immediate supply. In small kitchens solemn pigtailed daughters helped depressed mothers to perform the primitive ritual of its preparation. On the breakfast-tables of cheerless parlours it was partaken of in silence. Once the womenfolk discovered that it was thoroughly unpalatable, their zeal in forcing it on their households knew no bounds. 'You haven't eaten your Filboid Studge!' would be screamed at the appetiteless clerk as he hurried weariedly from the breakfast-table, and his evening meal would be prefaced by a warmed-up mess which would be explained as 'your Filboid Studge that you didn't eat this morning'. Those strange fanatics who ostentatiously mortify themselves, inwardly and outwardly, with health biscuits and health garments, battened aggressively on the new food. Earnest spectacled young men devoured it on the steps of the National Liberal Club. A bishop who did not believe in a future state preached against the poster, and a peer's daughter died from eating too much of the compound. A further advertisement was obtained when an infantry regiment mutinied and shot its officers rather than eat the nauseous mess; fortunately, Lord Birrel of Blatherstone, who was War Minister at the moment, saved the situation by his happy epigram, that 'Discipline to be effective must be optional.'

Filboid Studge had become a household word; but Dullamy wisely realised that it was not necessarily the last word in breakfast dietary; its supremacy would be challenged as soon as some yet more unpalatable food should be put on the market. There might even be a reaction in favour of something tasty and appetising, and the Puritan austerity of the moment might be banished from domestic cookery. At an opportune moment, therefore, he sold out his interests in the article which had brought him in colossal wealth at a critical juncture, and placed his financial reputation beyond the reach of cavil. As for Leonore, who was now an heiress on a far greater scale than ever before, he naturally found her something a vast deal higher in the husband market than a two-hundred-a-year poster designer. Mark Spayley, the brainmouse who had helped the financial lion with such untoward effect, was left to curse the day he produced the wonder-working poster.

'After all,' said Clovis, meeting him shortly afterwards at his club, 'you have this doubtful consolation, that 'tis not in mortals to countermand success.'

Activities

Parodies: *Jane Eyre*, 'Miss Mix', 'The Pig on Ted Hughes' and *Pride and Porringers*

1   In the parodies that you have read, you need to explore
    how far the writer has identified and exaggerated
    features of the original. Look at the texts again to check
    how they parody the original. You may also like to
    compare *Pride and Porringers* with *Pride and Prejudice*
    (page 12). The chart will help you to make a comparison
    with the original text.

Feature	Description/ example from from original text	Description/ example from parody
Events		
Description of characters		
Use of settings		
Language imagery		
Sentence structure/style		
Use of dialogue		
Attitudes and beliefs		

2 Choose an extract from this anthology or a different text with obvious stylistic features and try to write a parody. You can use the chart as a planning tool, and the advice on imitation in 'On Imitation' (page 188) may help you.

BADvertising/Adbusters

1 Consider how the BADverts get us to look afresh at images in advertising.

2 BADvertising relies on the contrast between the image sold and the reality. Through offering alternative images, it makes us question what we are being sold.

Example

Look at the *Perfect Recess* advert.

Here are some thoughts about the ways in which the contrasting images work:

Recess	Smoking
Recess or breaktime is the fun part of the day when kids relax.	Cigarettes are sold as a perfect way to relax.
Kids like to do things together.	Selling smoking to teenagers often relies on peer pressure to be cool.

The BADvert highlights the way cigarette companies benefit from peer pressure in schools.

Now choose two further examples to analyse.

3 Further activity: Using the guidelines 'How to create your own print ad' from Adbusters, create your own alternative advertising campaign. Plan using the guideline headings, and include the planning process when you present your work.

'Filboid Studge, the Story of the Mouse that Helped'

1 This short story both satirises big business and advertising, and subverts the conventions of fairy tales. Consider these two outlines:

A lion has a thorn stuck in its paw and is in dreadful pain. To his amazement a brave little mouse offers to help, and manages to gnaw the thorn away, even though this could be very dangerous. The lion is grateful and befriends the mouse.

A poor young man wants to marry a princess. He is set a seemingly impossible task to complete. To everyone's surprise, he does this successfully – he is richly rewarded and he marries the princess.

What is the moral?

2 Now read the story again. How has the fairy tale basis been subverted? What is the moral of Saki's story? What point is he making about the business world?

3 Filboid Studge commercials:

a Product names are important. What is conveyed by the name 'Pipenta'? Why did Mark change it to 'Filboid Studge'?

b Look at the descriptions of Mark Spayley's advertisements for the breakfast cereal.

c Make a note of the adjectives Saki uses to create the sombre pictures.

d What psychology does Spayley use in his campaign?

e What is suggested about the British character through the little scenes he describes?

4 Try writing your own subverted fairy tale with a modern setting, that makes a point about modern life. For example, would a modern Sleeping Beauty be woken up, or should she stop dozing around and get on with life?

5 Try to create Spayley's advertisements from the descriptions.

6 Devise an advertising campaign on the same principles, of making a product seem like an unpleasant duty.

Section 6
Something to Declare

I have nothing to declare except my genius.
Oscar Wilde (at the New York Customs House)

This section contains extracts which demonstrate how important outward signs of identity can be – the clothes you wear, the music you listen to, the things you own and the car you drive. You will be exploring how writers use these to suggest important things about their characters or themselves, and also considering the significance of these 'signs'.

It is important to be aware that fashions change. Remember that black jeans/polo shirts/The Smiths all had their day...

Extract 6.1: 'Kit Bag', *Moon Country* by Simon Armitage

'Kit Bag' is the opening of an account of Armitage's travels to Iceland, entitled *Moon Country*.

Personal

1 pair Line 7 blue/grey 'Light-trek' Gortex walking boots; 1 pair dark-brown three-hole ankle-length Doctor Martens: both size 9; 12 pairs M&S black cotton-rich socks; 12 pairs assorted M&S undies, boxer shorts & briefs; 1 pkt travel-size washing powder (biological); 3 × black Levi's 615s; 1 two-inch leather belt with silver buckle; 1 pair blue Troll leggings to double as long-johns; 5 × white + 5 × black XL Banana Republic 100% heavy cotton T-shirts; 4 × assorted button-down check shirts, Bronx Clothing, Huddersfield; 1 plain black all-occasion lightweight jacket; 1 hurricane-proof zip-up anorak with detachable hood.

Sony Walkman WM-FX43 plus Boots HE-6 in-ear headphones plus Sony SRS-18 mini-speaker system plus 12 Ever-Ready Energiser 1.5v alkaline batteries; 200ml silver hip flask plus contents; 35mm 1:4 Olympus Trip MD plus 12 rolls Kodak Tri-x film; silver/gold Parker 8mm roller-ball pen plus refill; Boots 'Notebook' series A4 and A6 hardback notebooks; 18-function Swiss army knife; book of matches; length of string; 1 Slazenger tennis ball; *National Geographic*; *NME*; *TLS*; *Letters from Iceland*.

Naked – Talking Heads; *Boy Child* – Scott Walker; *Debut* – Bjork; *Hatful of Hollow* – The Smiths; *The Infotainment Scan* – The Fall; *Swoon* – Prefab Sprout; *Blonde on Blonde/Bringing It All Back Home/Bootleg Series* – Dylan; *Document* – REM; *Absolute Classic*

Masterpieces – Felt. *Doolittle* – The Pixies; *It's a Shame about Ray* – The Lemonheads; Selected slim volumes – nothing over 50pp p/b and/or 3oz.

Gillette Cool Wave shaving gel with advanced lubricants for unsurpassed razor glide; pkt 10 Gillette Blue II Plus Lubrastrip; Sure Super-Dry anti-perspirant deodorant for men; Kouros Tonique Après Rasage 1.6 fl. oz. atomiser. 1 × 100ml tube Mentadent P with fluoride; Mentadent 'Diagonal' toothbrush, red and white; 75mg indomethacin slow-release capsules, one to be taken nightly or after food; 1 pkt Crooke's Sea-Legs as approved by St John's Ambulance; pkt ten Lemsip sachets, original flavour; 1 btl approx. 100 paracetamol (contents may settle during transit); Sainsbury's Lipsave lip balm, 1 stick; 1 tube 'quickactin'' Tinactin athlete's foot cream; Denman 5″ hairbrush with nylon bristles; Alberto Vo5 Power hair gel, for mega hold and total control.

EC passport; documentation and ticketing; BBC statement of intent and declaration of property; Icelandic Tourist Board 'waiver' in Icelandic; 30-page itinerary plus notes and required reading; credit cards; Eurocheques; cash and assorted ullage.

Perpetual Almanac of Saints and Folklore Diary.

Technical
Big black tape-recorder; little blue tape-recorder; microphone with fun-fur cover; microphone with sticky bit on back; black and red wires; tapes; batteries plus charger (labelled 'Batteries' and 'Charger'); instruction manuals × 5.

Extract 6.2: *High Fidelity* by Nick Hornby

In the extracts from this book Rob, the hero and narrator, shows how important clothes and music are to him, and has to reconsider his judgements.

Sixteen

This man comes into the shop to buy the Fireball XL5 theme tune for his wife's birthday (and I've got one, an original, and it's his for a tenner). And he's maybe two or three years younger than me, but he's well-spoken, and he's wearing a suit, and he's dangling his car keys and for some reason these three things make me feel maybe two decades younger than him, twenty or so to his fortysomething. And I suddenly have this burning desire to find out what he thinks of me. I don't give in to it, of course ('There's your change, there's your record, now come on, be honest, you think I'm a waster, don't you?'), but I think about it for ages afterwards, what I must look like to him.

I mean, he's married, which is a scary thing, and he's got the sort of car keys that you jangle confidently, so he's obviously got, like, a BMW or a Batmobile or something flash, and he does work which requires a suit, and to my untutored eye it looks like an expensive suit. I'm a bit smarter than usual today – I've got my newish black denims on, as opposed to my ancient blue ones, and I'm wearing a long-sleeved polo shirt thing that I actually went to the trouble of ironing – but even so I'm patently not a grown-up man in a grown-up job. Do I want to be like him: Not really, I don't think. But I find myself worrying away at that stuff about pop music again, whether I like it because I'm unhappy, or whether I'm unhappy because I like it. It would help me to know whether this guy has ever taken it seriously, whether he has ever sat surrounded by thousands and thousands of songs about... about... (say it, man, say it)... well, about love. I would guess that he hasn't. I would also guess Douglas Hurd hasn't, and the guy at the Bank of England hasn't; nor has David Owen or Nicholas Witchell or Kate Adie or loads of other famous people that I should be able to name, probably, but can't, because they never played for Booker T and the MGs. These people look as though they wouldn't have had the time to listen to the first side of *Al Green's Greatest Hits*, let alone all his other stuff (ten albums on the Hi label alone, although only nine of them were produced by Willie Mitchell); they're too busy fixing base rates and trying to bring peace to what was formerly Yugoslavia to listen to Sha La La (Make Me Happy)'.

So they might have the jump on me when it comes to accepted notions of seriousness (although as everyone knows, *Al Green Explores Your Mind* is as serious as life gets), but I ought to have the edge on them when it comes to matters of the heart. 'Kate,' I should be able to say, 'it's all very well dashing off to war zones. But what are you going to do about the only thing that really matters? You *know* what I'm talking about, baby.' And then I could give her all the emotional advice I gleaned from the College of Musical Knowledge. It hasn't worked out like that, though. I don't know anything about Kate Adie's love life, but it can't be in a worse state than mine, can it? I've spent nearly thirty years listening to people singing about broken hearts and has it helped me any?

So maybe what I said before, about how listening to too many records messes your life up... maybe there's something in it after all. David Owen, he's married, right? He's taken care of all that, and now he's a big-shot diplomat. The guy who came into the shop with the suit and the car keys, he's married too, and now he's, I don't know, a *businessman*. Me, I'm unmarried – at the moment as unmarried as it's possible to be – and I'm the owner of a failing record shop. It seems to me that if you place music (and books, probably, and films, and plays, and anything that makes you *feel*) at the centre of your being, then you can't afford to sort out your love life, start to think of it as the finished product. You've got to pick at it, keep it alive and in turmoil, you've got to pick at it and unravel it until it all comes apart and you're compelled to start all over again. Maybe we all live life at too high a pitch, those of us who absorb emotional things all day, and as a consequence we can never feel merely *content*: we have to be unhappy, or ecstatically, head-over-heels happy, and those states are difficult to achieve within a stable, solid relationship. Maybe Al Green is directly responsible for more than I ever realised.

See, records have helped me to fall in love, no question. I hear something new, with a chord change that melts my guts, and before I know it I'm looking for someone, and before I know it I've found her. I fell in love with Rosie after I'd fallen in love with a Cowboy Junkies song: I played it and played it and played it, and it made me dreamy, and I needed someone to dream about, and I found her, and… well, there was trouble.

Twenty-eight

About two weeks in, after a lot of talking and a tolerable amount of arguing, we go for dinner with Laura's friends Paul and Miranda. This might not sound very exciting to you, but it's a really big deal to me: it's a vote of confidence, an endorsement, a sign to the world that I'm going to be around for a few months at least. Laura and I have never seen eye-to-eye about Paul and Miranda, not that I've ever met either of them. Laura and Paul joined the law firm around the same time, and they got on well, so when she (and I) were asked round, I refused to go. I didn't like the sound of him, nor Laura's enthusiasm for him, although when I heard that there was a Miranda I could see I was being stupid, so I made up a load of other stuff. I said that he sounded typical of the sort of people she was going to be meeting all the time now she had this flash new job, and I was being left behind, and she got cross, so I upped the ante and attributed to him a hoity-toity voice and a whole set of interests and attitudes he probably hasn't got, and then Laura got *really* cross and went on her own. Paul and I had got off on the wrong foot, and when Laura invited them round to ours I went out until two in the morning just to make sure I didn't bump into them, even though they've got a kid and I knew they'd be gone by half past eleven. So when Laura said we'd been invited again I knew it was a big deal, not only because she was prepared to give it another go, but because it meant she'd been saying stuff about us living together again, and the stuff she'd been saying couldn't have been all bad.

As we stand on the doorstep of their house (nothing swanky, a three-bedroomed terraced in Kensal Green), I fiddle with the fly button on my 501s, a nervous habit that Laura strongly disapproves of, for perhaps understandable reasons. But tonight she looks at me and smiles, and gives my hand (my other hand, the one that isn't scrabbling frantically at my groin) a quick squeeze, and before I know it we're in the house amid a flurry of smiles and kisses and introductions.

Paul is tall and good-looking, with long (untrendy, can't-be-bothered-to-have-it-cut, computer-nerdy long, as opposed to hairdressery long) dark hair and a shadow that's nearer six-thirty than five o'clock. He's wearing a pair of old brown cords and a Body Shop T-shirt depicting something green, a lizard or a tree or a vegetable or something. I wish a few of the buttons on my fly were undone, just so I wouldn't feel overdressed. Miranda, like Laura, is wearing a baggy jumper and leggings, and a pair of pretty cool rimless specs, and she's blonde and round and pretty, not quite Dawn French round, but round enough for you to notice straight away. So I'm not intimidated by the clothes, or by the house, or the people, and anyway the people are so nice to me that for a moment I almost feel a bit weepy: it's obvious to even the most insecure that Paul and Miranda are delighted that I am here, either because they have decided that I am a Good Thing, or because Laura has told them that she is happy with the way things are (and if I've got it all wrong, and they're just acting, then who cares anyway, when the actors are this good?).

There isn't any what-would-you-call-your-dog stuff, partly because everyone knows what everyone does (Miranda is an English lecturer at an FE college), and partly because the evening isn't like that for a moment. They ask about Laura's dad, and Laura tells them about the funeral, or at least some of it, and also some stuff I didn't know – like, she says she felt a little thrill, momentarily, before all the pain and the grief and everything hit her – 'Like, God, this is the most grown up thing that's ever happened to me.'

And Miranda talks a bit about her mum dying, and Paul and I ask questions about that, and Paul and Miranda ask questions about my mum and dad, and then it all somehow moves on from there to aspirations, and what we want, and what we're not happy about, and... I don't know. It sounds stupid to say it, but despite what we're talking about, I really enjoy myself – I don't feel afraid of anybody, and whatever I say people take seriously, and I catch Laura looking fondly at me from time to time, which helps morale. It's not like anyone says any one thing that's memorable, or wise, or acute; it's more a mood thing. For the first time in my life I felt as though I'm in an episode of *Thirtysomething* rather than an episode of... of... of some sitcom that hasn't been made yet about three guys who work in a record shop and talk about sandwich fillings and sax solos all day, and I love it. And I know *Thirtysomething* is soppy and clichéd and American and naff, I can see that. But when you're sitting in a one-bedroom flat in Crouch End and your business is going down the toilet and your girlfriend's gone off with the guy from the flat upstairs, a starring role in a real-life episode of *Thirtysomething*, with all the kids and marriages and jobs and barbecues and k.d. lang CDs that this implies, seems more than one could possibly ask of life.

The first time I had a crush on anyone was four or five years before Alison Ashworth came along. We were on holiday in Cornwall, and a couple of honeymooners had the next breakfast table to us, and we got talking to them, and I fell in love with both of them. It wasn't one or the other, it was the unit. (And now I come to think about it, it was maybe these two as much as Dusty Springfield that gave me unrealistic expectations about relationships.) I think that each was trying, as newlyweds sometimes do, to show that they were brilliant with kids, that he'd make a brilliant dad and she'd make a fantastic mum, and I got the benefit of it: they took me swimming and rockpooling, and they bought me Sky Rays, and when they left I was heartbroken.

It's kind of like that tonight, with Paul and Miranda. I fall in love with both of them – with what they have, and the way they treat each other, and the way they make me feel as if I am the new centre of their world. I think they're great, and I want to see them twice a week every week for the rest of my life.

Only right at the end of the evening do I realise that I've been set up. Miranda's upstairs with their little boy; Paul's gone to see whether there's any ropy holiday liqueurs mouldering in the back of a cupboard anywhere, so that we can stoke up the log-fire glow we all have in our stomachs.

'Go and look at their records,' says Laura.

'I don't have to. I am capable of surviving without turning my nose up at other people's record collections, you know.'

'Please. I want you to.'

So I wander over to the shelf, and turn my head on one side and squint, and sure enough, it's a disaster area, the sort of CD collection that is so poisonously awful that it should be put in a steel case and shipped off to some Third World waste dump. They're all there: Tina Turner, Billy Joel, Kate Bush, Pink Floyd, Simply Red, the Beatles, of course, Mike Oldfield (*Tubular Bells I* and *II*), Meat Loaf… I don't have much time to examine the vinyl, but I see a couple of Eagles records, and I catch a glimpse of what looks suspiciously like a Barbara Dickson album.

Paul comes back into the room.

'I shouldn't think you approve of many of those, do you?'

'Oh, I don't know. They were a good band, the Beatles.'

He laughs. 'We're not very up on things, I'm afraid. We'll have to come into the shop, and you can put us right.'

'Each to his own, I say.'

Laura looks at me. 'I've never heard you say it before. I thought "each to his own" was the kind of sentiment that'd be enough to get you hung in the brave new Fleming world.'

I manage a crooked smile, and hold out my brandy glass for some ancient Drambuie out of a sticky bottle.

'You did that deliberately,' I say to her on the way home. 'You knew all along I'd like them. It was a trick.'

'Yeah. I tricked you into meeting some people you'd think were great. I conned you into having a nice evening.'

'You know what I mean.'

'Everybody's faith needs testing from time to time. I thought it would be amusing to introduce you to someone with a Tina Turner album, and then see whether you still felt the same.'

I'm sure I do. Or at least, I'm sure I will. But tonight, I have to confess (but only to myself, obviously) that maybe, given the right set of peculiar, freakish, probably unrepeatable circumstances, it's not what you like but what you're like that's important. I'm not going to be the one that explains to Barry how this might happen, though.

Extract 6.3: 'Deeper Than Colour' by Ijeoma Inyama

This story is about superficial differences disguising underlying attraction between two teenagers.

God! Miss Halpern, our English teacher, is well renk! She reckons our class would be '*much more productive*' if we weren't sat with our friends. So she moves us about and makes us sit with people she *knows* we'd never sit with through choice. She's vex me *twice*, man! First of all, you don't expect to get treated like a first year when you're in the *fifth* year – I mean, her idea of a seating arrangement is well antiquated! And secondly, she's taken me from my spars, man! Ever since the second year, I've sat next to Heather Phillips, in front of Antoinette Varley and Takesha Brown. Now barely into the first term of the fifth and we get split up!

'Nadine Charles, I want you to sit next to John Danucci in front of my desk.'

Now she's vexed me four times, no, make that five. Sitting next to Danucci *and* in the front row. I can't believe it! Neither can the rest of the class. *Everyone* knows we're the worst pairing ever.

Let me explain some simple rudimentary classroom psychology, while I grab up my books and cuss my way down the aisle. See, I'm no roughneck, but I love my ragga and jungle… like the girls I go round with – Heather, Antoinette and Takesha. So naturally we get friendly with like-minded guys. Horace Batchelor's an example. 'Cept for Horace, the guys ain't true ragamuffins, but they do get a roughneck reputation 'cause they like ragga. Being Black helps. And if you can run the lyrics… well, you're talking god-like status.

But let me get back to Danucci. He hangs out with the 'trendies'. We call them the *Kiss FM posse*. They're into

'British soul' and buy their clothes from 'Hyper' – anything that's the latest t'ing. I mean, if it was thrashing two dustbin lids together, them lot'd be into that, no danger. So, us lot stick to ourselves, them lot do likewise – and never the twain shall meet stylee. I mean, if I went to some roughneck ragga sound dressed like them freaky deakies – some Barbarella meets and rough up Miss Marple kind of doo-lah I'd get nuff comments!

It must sound like something out of *West Side Story*, the Jets versus the Sharks. But it ain't. We don't have gang fights. Just a mutual understanding that we don't have nothing to do with each other. And that's why me and Danucci are the worst pairing Miss Halpern could have made.

A ragga-loving, hardcore jungle *gyal* ain't got nothing decent to say to a trendy freaky deaky.

At morning break my situation is the focus of the playground discussion. Horace reckons that Miss Halpern needs '*hormone treatment*', or a good kick up the backside, or both, for what she's done. Then he hits on me! '…and don't get no ideas!'

'Yeah, and I'm *really* your girlfriend, ain't I?' I snap. 'Besides, I couldn't go out with no freaky deakster. I'd be too shamed up to walk down the street with him!

Horace has asked me out twice and twice I've turned him down. Truth is, I'd be too shamed up to walk down the street with *him*! I can't stand the way he's always got to have a comb in his miserable head – but does he ever use it? Now OK, I wouldn't get on the cover of *Black Hair & Beauty* (Takesha could easy), but I could sneak in between. So what makes a guy with no class, style, the personality of a crusty old pair of Y-fronts and looks that would make Godzilla a hunk think that I'd be interested in him? Try and explain that to Horace Batchelor. I've tried, but he won't listen. He reckons I'm the one for him. God knows why.

Two weeks and six English lessons have passed and I'm still sitting next to Danucci. I give him dirty looks, run down *Kiss FM* loud enough for him to hear and make sure my books cover at least half his desk. He ain't said a word to me. Maybe he's scared of Horace. But it really annoys me 'cause it's like I'm not there! He shares jokes and raves about the latest rare groove with his trendy pals – and they all sit around me, which I can't stand. And he exchanges loving glances with his girlfriend, Debra Haynes. She sits in the back row, two seats away from Heather. You've got to see this girl. She thinks she's *it*, her nose up in the air or looking down it at you. She's well facety! She thinks she's so hip in her clothes, but she always looks like she's wearing the clothes her grandmother gave her; which is probably the case.

Well, all that I can I take. But then today Miss Halpern tells us she wants us to write a short story based on some aspect of our lives. Creative writing's got to be the thing I hate most. I get bored after writing one line! Anyway, she goes on and on about how she wants us to use '*...research as a means of getting information about your backgrounds...*'. Which really means, bug your parents for the next seven days. I can't be bothered with all that. But Danucci and his crew think it's a great idea. Typical!

On our way home from school that afternoon, a crowd of us stopped by the newsagent's, ignoring the ten-foot-high sign that reads 'ONLY TWO KIDS AT A TIME'. And Danucci's in there with a couple of his trendy mates.

Hassle time!

Horace accidentally-on-purpose knocks into Danucci, whose nose is stuck in a music magazine. Danucci don't even glance up – Horace is well miffed. Then Takesha shoves me into Danucci and he almost drops the magazine. He glares at me. I'd never noticed his sparkling green eyes, his curly black eyelashes and…

'Nadine!'

My friends are all looking at me like I've grown a moustache or something. Danucci goes up to the counter with his mates to pay for the magazine. But not before giving me a look that could've had me ten foot under. For the first time I realise that he hates me as much as I hate him.

Talk about stress me out! I've got Miss Halpern on my back about that stupid short story I haven't written. Heather, Antoinette and Takesha on my back about fancying Danucci, and Horace on my back about going out with him. Well, before I crack up, I'm going to have one last go at getting some order into my life. '*Deal with each problem one at a time*' is my mum's favourite saying. First on my list is getting that story written.

Normally, I never go near a library. Man, I break out in a cold sweat just thinking about one! But I force myself. The assignment's due in on Thursday and that's tomorrow! So in I go, on my own. I could've gone in with Antoinette and Takesha, as they love the library, but they'd already done their assignments. Heather *never* does assignments and she has the same aversion to libraries as I do – serious intellectual atmosphere, ugh!

I go straight upstairs to the study area. There are 'nuff kids in here, man! Swotting at the *beginning* of term? That's well sad, man! It's hunt for a seat time. I make my way past the tables. *No one was talking*. Can you believe that? Noses stuck in books. Disgusting! Ah-ha, a seat right by the window at the back. I could get away with eating my Mars bar without the crusty librarian seeing me. A freckle-faced, ginger-haired girl heads towards my seat. I throw myself into it. She gives me a filthy look and stomps off.

So I get out my exercise book and my Biros and take in the other kids around the table. Sangita, who's in the year below me; she lives in the library apparently. Tunde, a really quiet guy in my year – and the cleverest, Cheryl Watson, also in my year and a bookworm and… oh no! Danucci!

It's too late to move – there's nowhere else to sit. So I stay there silently cursing myself – 'til he looks up and sees me. (He'd had his head down in a computer book. That assignment's not due in 'til next month!) He kind of scowls at me, then returns to his book.

I can't concentrate on my story – it's that awkward. Ten minutes have gone by without us saying a word. This is driving me mad! I've got to say something!

'Look, I'm sorry about the other day in the newsagent's, but it weren't my fault.'

He looks at me, stunned, like he must've been preparing himself for aggro or something, particularly since none of his friends is around. But he still doesn't say anything.

'I said, I apologise. What d'you want, blood?' I hate being made to feel uncomfortable.

'Why?'

I can't work the boy out. 'Why what?'

'Why are you saying you're sorry when we both know you don't mean it?'

'Hey, you ain't in my head, so you don't know what's going on in there. But if you must know, I don't never say nothing that I don't mean. "*Better to offend than pretend*" is my motto.'

He folds his arms across his chest, looking triumphant. 'Not so hard without your mates, eh?'

'Neither are you.'

'I don't bother you, but you're *always* bothering me.'

A librarian near by tells us to be quiet, so we are for

about half a minute. Then he goes: 'Is that your English assignment?'

I stop doodling on the page. 'Nah, I'm designing a hi-tech kitchen for my mum's birthday present.'

The librarian is glowering at us.

'So what's it going to be about?' Danucci asks.

'How the hell do I know?'

He's getting as narked as I am, and I feel my conscience prickling…

'I don't know what to write,' I whisper. 'I don't know *how* to write.'

'It's easy. Write about what you know.'

'Oh yeah? As easy as that? So what did you write about then?'

So Danucci tells me his short story. But he has to tell me outside 'cause we get kicked out.

Massimo, the guy in his story, is about eight or nine. He teases – no – bullies is more like it, his next-door neighbour's son Haresh, who's around two years younger. He'd call him 'paki' and stuff 'cause that's what all his friends at school did, bully Black and Asian kids. It was a mainly White school. Anyway, one day, Massimo's grandad Alfonso (I love the names) came to visit, overheard the name-calling and abuse and ordered Massimo inside. Alfonso told Massimo how hard it was for him being an Italian immigrant in the late thirties and forties because of Mussolini and that and also because he was well dark, being Sicilian. He told Massimo that he was shaming him by insulting Haresh. Massimo felt really bad because he loved his grandad (basically because he spoilt him rotten). Then Massimo ended up in a secondary school which was racially mixed and he had no problem forming friendships which rivalled the UN in their racial and cultural diversity.

'Our school's nothing like the UN.'

'So you guessed Massimo is based on me.'

'Just call me Einstein.'

He laughs.

'There's no way I could write like that.'

'Sure you can. Write about what you know.'

I look at him. 'I don't get it. Why are you helping me?'

He's about to answer when I spot my spars coming out of McDonald's. I freeze. Danucci sighs. 'You want me to disappear, right?'

They'll see us any time soon. So I goes, 'Well, you'd do the same.'

He's got that same look he had in the newsagent's. 'Would I?' And he crosses the street in a huff just as they spot me.

The past three days have been a bummer, an all-time low. Oh, I got my assignment done and handed it in on time, no worries there. Except that it's crap. No, it's my friends that have been stressing me out – big time – with the Danucci thing. They've been saying that I'll be trading in Redrat for Jamiroquai. Yesterday, Horace got me so vexed that I cussed him about his nappy-never-see-comb head. As for Danucci, he won't so much as look at me. Worst of all, that's what's bugging me the most! I know now why I hated him so much. I was *making* myself hate him because I knew I *liked* him. But now with him ignoring me I feel so depressed I can't eat or sleep let alone think properly.

Enough is enough! I'm going to sort this mess out. So I write him a note and put it in his desk before English class. If he still wants to know, he'll meet me by the huts after class.

'Ain't you afraid to be seen in public with me?'

I shrug my shoulders. I know he's pleased I left him that note. His green eyes are twinkling like crazy.

'I want to apologise.'

'Like last time?'

'You're making this really difficult.'

He leans against the wall. 'Good. You really narked me off the other day.'

'I know and I've been suffering since.'

'Friends giving you a hard time?'

'*You're* giving me a hard time.'

Silence. I count the stripes on my hi-tops; one, two, three...

'I've always liked you Nadine.' He says it so softly.

'I'd never have guessed.'

'And as you wrote me a note...'

'Yeah, I like you, too. I guess I was trying to hide it by giving you a hard time.'

He smiles at me. 'I ain't saying it's going to be easy if we're friendly-like, my friends'll give me a hard time, too, you know. But I would never cross the street if they saw me with you. It depends on how much you want to be part of the crowd.'

'I've been really miserable since that day, I feel like I'd be living a lie if I kept... you know, pretending.'

'Better to offend than pretend, right?'

'Is Debra Haynes your girlfriend?'

He shakes his head. 'Is Horace Batchelor your boyfriend?'

I roll my eyes.

Then he pulls me close to him and we kiss. Then he puts his arm around me as we head towards the playground, where everyone will see us! I ain't going to lie and say I feel a hundred per cent comfortable about it. But for my own piece of mind, I've got to give it a go. Especially since I've just written a short story about it. I mean, it's got to be a first in our school: a ragga-loving junglis girl going with a trendy freaky deak.

Activities

'Kit Bag' from *Moon Country*

1   What does the writer reveal about himself and his attitudes through possessions?

2   Read 'Kit Bag' again and consider the following points.

   a What does Armitage suggest about himself through his clothes/where he shops?

   b What do the possessions listed in the second paragraph tell us about him?

   c Why do you think he has given details of his music?

   d The fourth paragraph contains more than a hint of irony. What do you think is his attitude to consumer slogans? What is he suggesting by listing all these toiletries among his luggage yet mocking them?

   e Look at the final section headed 'Technical'. What is Armitage suggesting about his interest in/competency with technical items? How does he do this?

   f Analyse the structure of the sentences. How does this differ from continuous prose?

   g Look at the organisation of the paragraphs – would this necessarily be changed if written in continuous prose?

3   Create a list of luggage items that reveal what you like *and* what you're like.

4   Look at a description of a character from a book you have studied, and analyse the way the author creates impressions through details about clothes/possessions.

5   There is an element of self-mockery in both 'Kit Bag' and 'Things My Girlfriend and I Have Argued About' (page 18). Can you identify how it is achieved in each?

High Fidelity

1   Look again at Chapter 16 in the extract. Consider the
    following points.

    a How does he judge the man who comes into the shop
       to buy a record?

    b How does Rob contrast himself with this man?

2   Music has clearly always been very important to Rob –
    now he is beginning to re-examine his priorities. Look
    again at the text.

    a How is his confusion shown?

    b How is it suggested that he sees himself as immature?

3   In Chapter 28 of the extract, again we see Rob exhibiting
    the same sorts of fears and judgements. Find examples of
    his reactions to other people's:

    • jobs
    • clothes
    • houses
    • music.

4   In both extracts, Rob describes what he is wearing. Why
    do you think he does this?

5   Rob feels that the evening is a sort of test set by his
    girlfriend – a test of his attitudes and maturity.

    a Why does she tell him to look at their records?

    b How does he react to their taste in music? Why do
       you think the writer gives us details of their albums?

    c What realisation has Rob come to by the end of the
       evening? Has he passed the 'test'?

6   Language: This novel is written in an informal,
    conversational tone. Try to identify some features of
    language and sentence structure that are more typical of
    spoken than formal, written English.

7 Comparisons: Compare the tone in *High Fidelity* to that in 'Things My Girlfriend and I Have Argued About' (page 18). In what ways are they similar?

8 Discuss as a group whether you think that relaxing your opinions about obsessions is an inevitable part of growing up? Or do you think that people just look for a different range of identity 'signs'?

'Deeper Than Colour'

1 Language is important in establishing the character's identity – create a glossary of all the teenage slang in the story which explains the meaning.

2 Why do you think the author has chosen to use this slang rather than write in more formal, standard English? Think about the intended audience, and the author's underlying purpose.

3 Clothes and music are clearly important to the identity of the teenagers here. Make a chart like that below with details that identify each group.

	Ragamuffins	Trendies
Music		
Clothes		
Names		
Work		

4 Nadine and Horace have a lot in common in terms of their group identity, but she is not attracted to him despite this. What does this suggest?

5 Compare the ways in which Horace and Danucci are described.

6 What does Danucci's story suggest about his attitudes?

7 Nadine is clearly an honest person who is open to having her mind changed. What suggests this earlier in the story?

8 What has Nadine learned by the end of the story?

9 As a group discuss the following.

   a Compare Nadine's experience with that of Rob in *High Fidelity*.

   b Look at the story's title. What expectations does it create?

   c The story is about superficial differences that make people judge each other – what link does the author suggest with racial attitudes?

10 Look at the glossary of teenage slang you compiled in question 1.

   a Choose a passage from a work of classic literature from this anthology or another book, and re-write it in teen-speak.

   b What changes do you notice? Does the teenage language fit with the subject/period? Does your version make it more relevant, or simply funny? If the latter, what else needs changing? Setting? Time? Type of characters?

Section 7
Authors and Their Craft

'Fool,' said my Muse to me, 'look in thy heart and write.'
Sir Philip Sidney, 1554–1586

A Man may write at any time, if he will set himself doggedly to it.
Dr Samuel Johnson, 1709–1784

In this section you will find advice and activities from published writers. You can use these to explore and evaluate texts that you read, or to develop your own writing.

Extract 7.1: 'On Imitation' from *On Becoming a Writer* by Dorothy Brande

---

On Becoming a Writer by Dorothy Brande is a classic help text for aspiring writers – it has never been out of print since the 1930s. One reason for its continuing popularity is the practical nature of the writing tasks suggested.

Now as to imitation for practice. When you have learned to find in the writing of others the material which is suggestive for your own work, you are in a position to imitate in the only way in which imitation can be of any use to you. The philosophies, the ideas, the dramatic notions of other writers of fiction should not be directly adopted. If you find them congenial, go back to the sources from which those authors originally drew their ideas, if you are able to find them. There study the primary sources and take any items over into your own work only when they have your deep acquiescence – never because the author in whose work you find them is temporarily successful, or because another can use them effectively. They are yours to use only when you have made them your own by full acquaintance and acceptance.

Imitating Technical Excellences

But technical excellences can be imitated, and with great advantage. When you have found a passage, long or short, which seems to you far better than anything of the sort you are yet able to do, sit down to learn from it.

Study it even more closely than you have been studying your specimen book or specimen story as a whole. Tear it apart almost word by word. If possible, find a cognate passage in your own work to use for comparison. Let us assume, for instance, that you have trouble with that bugbear of most writers when they first begin to work seriously – conveying the passing of time. You either string out your story to no purpose, following your character through a number of unimportant or confusing activities to get him from one significant scene to another, or you drop him abruptly and take him up abruptly between two paragraphs. In the story you have been reading, which is about the length of the one you want to write, you find that the author has handled such transitions smoothly, writing just enough, but not a word too much, to convey the illusion of time's passing between two scenes. Well, then; how does he do it? He uses – how many words? Absurd as it may seem at first to think that anything can be learned by word-counting, you will soon realise that a good author has a just sense of proportion; he is artist enough to feel how much space should be given to take his character from the thick of action in one situation into the centre of the next.

How to Spend Words
In a story of five thousand words, let us say, your author has given a hundred and fifty words to the passing of a night and a day, rather unimportant, in the life of his hero. And you? Three words, or a sentence perhaps: 'The next day, Conrad, etc.'* Something too skimpy about it altogether. Or, on the other hand, although there was nothing in Conrad's night and morning that was pertinent to the story in hand, and although you have

---

*I hasten to say that there are occasions on which the words, 'The next day, Conrad, etc.,' may be exactly the number of words and exactly the emphasis to be given to a transition. We are assuming for the moment that such a transition is, for the story you are engaged in, too abrupt.

already used up all the space you can afford in the sketching of your hero's character, by sheer inability to stop talking about him once you have started you may have given six hundred or a thousand words to the retailing of totally irrelevant matters about his day.

How does the author expend the words that you have counted? Does he drop for a few paragraphs into indirection, after having told the story up to this time straightforwardly? Does he choose words which convey action, in order to show that his hero, although not engaged during that time in anything that furthered the story, still has a full life while he is, at it were, offstage? What clues does he drop into the concluding sentence which allows him to revert to the true action? When you have found as much as you are able to find in that way, write a paragraph of your own, imitating your model *sentence by sentence*.

Counteracting Monotony

Again it may be that you feel that your writing is monotonous, that verb follows noun, and adverb follows verb, with a deadly sameness throughout your pages. You are struck by the variety, the pleasant diversity of sentence structures and rhythms in the author you are reading. Here is the real method of playing the sedulous ape: The first sentence has twelve words; you will write a twelve word sentence. It begins with two words of one syllable each, the third is a noun of two syllables, the fourth is an adjective of four syllables, the fifth an adjective of three, etc. Write one with words of the same number of syllables noun for noun, adjective for adjective, verb for verb, being sure that the words carry their emphasis on the same syllables as those in the model. By choosing an author whose style is complementary to your own you can teach yourself a great deal about sentence formation and prose rhythm in this way. You will not wish, or need, to do it often, but to do it occasionally is remarkably helpful. You become aware of variation and tone in your reading, and learn as you read. Once having taken the trouble to analyse a sentence into its component parts and construct a similar one of your own, you will find that some part of your mind is thereafter awake to subtleties which you may have passed obliviously before.

Extract 7.2: 'The English Exam' by Joe Swarbrick

'The English Exam' was written by a Year 11 student about his experience of writing under exam conditions.

For two months the gym hall is not being used for sport. The weather is fine, so relocating to the great outdoors holds no problems for the lucky teachers spared the trial of invigilation. Instead, they supervise a fairly large game of rounders on the field we walk past on our way to the hall. The year nines, as yet untroubled by the horrors of coursework, modules, and The Most Important Three Hours of Your Life, frolic with hoots and cries of innocent joy. A mid-youth crisis looms: those days are over for us. From now on we are adults. The summer break seems a long way off.

Despite being a full twenty minutes early, the hall has already attracted a sizeable crowd of hysterically nervous students, the irony of course being that these are the ones with the least to worry about. These are the people with highly organised, carefully coloured-in revision timetables pinned to their walls like mission briefings in a war film. In their heads, a portly moustachioed general barks orders to re-read texts, study revision guides, make audio tapes of their notes, get plenty of sleep. The effect of this continual barking has pushed their sanity to the limits; they know they have just three hours in which to prove themselves to be the model students they have aspired to be over the last two years. They quiz each other with quickfire questions on onomatopoeia, pathetic fallacy, the sexuality of Iago, why most of the characters in *Of Mice and Men* begin with the letter C. Harebrain theories are flung around, adding to the tension, irritating like a swarm of wasps at a picnic. To balance this scene of intellectual hysteria, a group of boys are playing football. This activity is swiftly discarded in favour of throwing things. First drinks bottles, then pebbles, then large rocks which scatter the swarm of theories buzzing around the fire doors of the hall. It strikes me that it could be liberating to have such a lack of care for my future.

It is of course wise in a situation like this to avoid everyone in order to avoid being stung by either a rock or an idea. A calm approach is required: I only know what I know. I cannot change what is now in my head. I just hope to God that I can get it all out on paper. I am a boxer before a fight: psyching myself up, staying focused, my mind sharpened to a pinprick on what I am about to do. A chemistry teacher arrives, face unusually stern, dressed soberly if not funereally, and she opens the doors.

Bags and coats are placed at the front. Silence from now on. Texts are retrieved along with clutches of pens, clear plastic pencil cases and, in an alarming number of cases, large bags of sweets and clear bottles of drink. Where will they find the time to feast on this buffet of e-numbers? I intend to write in this exam. I spend a moment reflecting on the necessity for clear pencil cases and drinks bottles. If a student can realistically scribble an entire syllabus onto twenty square centimetres of canvas, then how hard can these exams actually be? The grid of tables momentarily confuses, but they are alphabetically arranged and I hunt out people whose surnames begin with an S. The massive hall slowly fills with students. Nervous energy is tangible. Stay focused. Eighteen-page answer booklets are handed out. Is that how much they expect us to write? My candidate number is printed alongside my name on the small rectangle of paper situated at the corner of the desk. I glance at it, but it is merely a precaution as we are already two weeks into the exams. Yet I mustn't leave anything to chance. Surname –

check. Other names – check. Date, subject, exam board – check, check, check. Easy so far. The name of the exam board arrives on the yellow exam paper which takes me by surprise as it hits my desk, deposited by a stoney-faced PE teacher; one of the unlucky ones. Nothing for him to do for the next three hours. He must watch us all, silently scouring the grid for unusual activity. Not like the mocks, where he could do some marking or read a magazine. This is not a drill.

Open your papers.

Now.

I flick deftly to the correct section, wasting no time. The tension has turned to adrenaline. The ghouls of blank minds and blind panic that had haunted me over the past months now evaporate from my mind, floating high up to the strip lights on the ceiling, perhaps ready to prey on some other unfortunate soul. The question is good. Calm but quick, the essay is planned with scribbles and underlining, annotations of texts are read, re-read, processed and contextualised. The conscious mind takes a break for a while as a more instinctive approach takes over. By Divine Osmosis, exactly how to write a good exam essay has become as natural as tying a shoelace. Five lines of introduction are proceeded by three healthy fifteen-line paragraphs and a neat double bow of a conclusion. Right on schedule, the essay is finished. Nothing can go wrong now. Images of glowing parents, raucous celebratory parties and, in the distant future, top-level degrees and high-salary jobs invade my head, momentarily replacing my concentration. Must not rest on my laurels. What's next?

Just don't panic. Just re-read the question. Again. It's OK, there's a choice. No. No no no no no no. I didn't revise that poem. I didn't like it, so I didn't revise it. I have no annotations. The ghouls plummet straight back into my cranium from their lofty position, tormenting the images of success. The adrenaline is working against me now. My eyes dart round quickly, taking in over a hundred students smugly scribbling. Yet instead of making me want to weep, this fuels me with a macho competitiveness. I shall answer this question! It is a test of my character! I can achieve anything! Pen is put to paper and slowly but surely a makeshift raft of an answer is constructed next to the spectacular cruise liner of before. A quick re-read of what I have done convinces me it is just about seaworthy.

Unfortunately, this little hiccup has left me with three-quarters of an hour to answer my final question. Confidently, the introduction is as short and to the point as a bullet. Yet every other sentence my eyes dart to the clock, which is moving far too quickly. Slowly, my handwriting is becoming more and more muddled, as is the complexity of my analysis. Big words instead of small. The paragraphs are shorter. I'm regressing back to childhood. Yet somewhere in my head a voice whispers a comforting mantra of 'point, quotation, explanation' which keeps the structure of my otherwise wild paragraphs in line. This is a true test. My hand aches but I keep on writing, my eyes now fixed on the page. I finished physics half an hour early. Was that good? Or have I messed that one up too? The chemistry teacher announces that we have five minutes left. Points left sloppily dragging are hastily double-knotted in a four-line conclusion, bringing the essay to a sharp close. A quick check for spelling, grammar and punctuation is curtailed by the PE teacher, who takes my papers from me into the sizeable pile hidden behind a large, tracksuited arm. And it is over.

Like some sort of Chinese torture, only in reverse. We are pulled slowly up off the large spike and set down on the floor. The process is almost pleasant; the weight is removed from our shoulders and put in the hands of somebody else. There is no control now. The summer is one step closer. The nervous theorisers compare answers, the rock throwers go to play football. I go home and watch television, and try not to think about the next one.

Extract 7.3: *Learning to Think* by Ted Hughes

Learning to Think is a book by poet Ted Hughes in which he attempts to explain the thinking processes behind his poetry writing. He offers ideas and exercises for teachers and individuals to develop their own poetry writing.

Now first of all I had better make it quite clear that I am going to talk about a certain kind of thinking. One of the odd wonderful things about this activity we call thinking is that to some extent everybody invents their own brand, has his own way of thinking, not only his own thoughts. You do not ever have to worry that you are not thinking properly – not unless you enter some very specialised job, where a very specialised kind of thinking is required. All you have to do really is think.

And thinking, as we know, is as natural as breathing – some sort of thinking is generally going on in us all the time. So what is all the fuss about? Well, the terrible fact is that though we are all more or less thinking of something or other all the time, some of us are thinking more and some less. Some of us are more energetic about it.

Just as some people are bustling about all the time, getting things done, while others just sit around – so it is inside people's minds – some brains are battling and working and remembering and puzzling things over all the time, or much of the time, and other brains are just lying down snoring and occasionally turning over. Now I am not speaking to that first kind. There is not much I can say to them except wish them good luck. It is to the lazy or secret minds that I am now speaking, and from my own experience I imagine this includes nineteen people out of every twenty. I am one of that clan myself and always have been.

At school, I was plagued by the idea that I really had much better thoughts than I could ever get into words. It was not that I could not find the words, or that the thoughts were too deep or too complicated for words. It was simply that when I tried to speak or write down the thoughts, those thoughts had vanished. All I had was a numb blank feeling, just as if somebody had asked me the name of Julius Caesar's eldest son, or said '7,283 times 6,956 – quick. Think, think, think'. Now for one reason or another I became very interested in thóse thoughts of mine that I could never catch. Sometimes they were hardly what you could call a thought – they were a dim sort of feeling about something. They did not fit into any particular subject – history or arithmetic or anything of that sort, except perhaps English. I had the idea, which gradually grew on me, that these were the right sort of thoughts for essays, and yet probably not even essays. But for the most part they were useless to me because I could never get hold of them. Maybe when I was writing an essay I got the tail end of one, but that was not very satisfying.

Now maybe you can see what was happening. I was thinking all right, and even having thoughts that seemed interesting to me, but I could not keep hold of the thoughts, or fish them up when I wanted them. I would think this fact was something peculiar to me, and of interest to nobody else, if I did not know that most people have the same trouble. What thoughts they have are fleeting thoughts – just a flash of it, then gone – or, though they know they know something, or have ideas about something, they just cannot dig those ideas up when they are wanted. Their minds, in fact, seem out of their reach. That is a curious thing to say, but it is quite true.

There is the inner life, which is the world of final reality, the world of memory, emotion, imagination, intelligence and natural common sense, and which goes on all the time, consciously or unconsciously, like the heart beat. There is also the thinking process by which we break into that inner life and capture answers and evidence to support the answers out of it. That process of raid, or persuasion, or ambush, or dogged hunting, or surrender, is the kind of thinking we have to learn and if we do not somehow learn it, then our minds lie in us like the fish in the pond of a man who cannot fish.

Now you see the kind of thinking I am talking about. Perhaps I ought not to call it thinking at all – it is just that we tend to call everything that goes on in our heads thinking. I am talking about whatever kind of trick or skill it is that enables us to catch those elusive or shadowy thoughts, and collect them together, and hold them still so we can get a really good look at them. I will illustrate what I mean with an example: If you were told, 'Think of your uncle' – how long could you hold the idea of your uncle in your head? Right, you imagine him. But then at once he reminds you of something else and you are thinking of that, he has gone into the background, if he has not altogether disappeared. Now get your uncle back. Imagine your uncle and nothing else – nothing whatsoever. After all, there is plenty to be going on with in your uncle, his eyes, what expression? His hair, where is it parted? How many waves has it? What is the exact shade? Or if he is bald, what does the skin feel like? His chin – just how is it? Look at it. As you can see, there is a great deal to your uncle – you could spend hours on him, if you could only keep him in your mind for hours; and when you have looked at him from head to foot, in your memory you have all the memories of what he has said and done, and all your own feelings about him and his sayings and doings. You could spend weeks on him, just holding him there in your mind, and examining the thoughts you have about him. I have exaggerated that, but you see straightaway that it is quite difficult to think about your uncle and nothing but your uncle for more than a few seconds. So how can you ever hope to collect all your thoughts about him.

At the same time you obviously could not do that with everything that came into your head – grip hold of it with your imagination, and never let it go till you had studied every grain of it. It would not leave you any time to live. Nevertheless, it is possible to do it for a time. I will illustrate the sort of thing I mean with a poem called *View of a Pig*. In this poem, the poet stares at something which is quite still, and collects the thoughts that concern it.

He does it quite rapidly and briefly, never lifting his eyes from the pig. Obviously, he does not use every thought possible – he chooses the thoughts that fit best together to make a poem. Here is the poem: *View of a Pig*.

> The pig lay on a barrow dead.
> It weighed, they said, as much as three men.
> Its eyes closed, pink white eyelashes.
> Its trotters stuck straight out.
>
> Such weight and thick, pink bulk
> Set in death seemed not just dead.
> It was less than lifeless, further off.
> It was like a sack of wheat.
>
> I thumped it without feeling remorse.
> One feels guilty insulting the dead,
> Walking on graves. But this pig
> Did not seem able to accuse.
>
> It was too dead. Just so much
> A poundage of lard and pork.
> Its last dignity had entirely gone.
> It was not a figure of fun.

Too dead now to pity.
To remember its life, din, stronghold
Of earthly pleasure as it had been,
Seemed a false effort, and off the point.

Too deadly factual. Its weight
Oppressed me – how could it be moved?
And the trouble of cutting it up!
The gash in its throat was shocking, but not pathetic.

Once I ran at a fair in the noise
To catch a greased piglet
That was faster and nimbler than a cat,
Its squeal was the rending of metal.

Pigs must have hot blood, they feel like ovens,
Their bite is worse than a horse's –
They chop a half-moon clean out.
They eat cinders, dead cats.

Distinctions and admirations such
As this one was long finished with.
I stared at it for a long time. They were going
   to scald it,
Scald it and scour it like a doorstep.

Now where did the poet learn to settle his mind like
that on to one thing? It is a valuable thing to be able to do
– but something you are never taught at school, and not
many people do it naturally. I am not very good at it, but
I did acquire some skill in it. Not in school, but while I was
fishing. I fished in still water, with a float. As you know, all
a fisherman does is stare at his float for hours on end. I
have spent hundreds and hundreds of hours staring at a
float – a dot of red or yellow the size of a lentil, ten yards

away. Those of you who have never done it might think it is a very drowsy pastime. It is anything but that.

All the little nagging impulses, that are normally distracting your mind, dissolve. They have to dissolve if you are to go on fishing. If they do not, then you cannot settle down: you get bored and pack up in a bad temper. But once they have dissolved, you enter one of the orders of bliss.

Your whole being rests lightly on your float, but not drowsily: very alert, so that the least twitch of the float arrives like an electric shock. And you are not only watching the float. You are aware, in a horizonless and slightly mesmerised way, like listening to the double bass in orchestral music, of the fish below there in the dark. At every moment your imagination is alarming itself with the size of the thing slowly leaving the weeds and approaching your bait. Or with the world of beauties down there, suspended in total ignorance of you. And the whole purpose of this concentrated excitement, in this arena of apprehension and unforeseeable events, is to bring up some lovely solid thing like living metal from a world where nothing exists but those inevitable facts which raise life out of nothing and return it to nothing.

Thinking of one thing like this is not the only way to tackle a problem or to raise your thoughts. Sometimes we want not just our thoughts about this thing, or that thing. We want the progress of thoughts – the way one follows another, as in a story or argument. In other words, we are not then concentrating on one point, but raising one point after another and concentrating on each in turn.

Perhaps you will see that this is the next step, lesson two, after acquiring the skill I have been describing. In a way, the poems that have been read belong to lesson one. It is a very simple lesson, but, as I have said, well worth learning.

Extract 7.4: *Screenwriting* by Raymond G. Frensham

Raymond G. Frensham is a freelance script adviser. This book is a guide for aspiring writers and teaches the skills of presentation and structure, as well as how to make the content of their work more interesting for film-makers. In this extract he concentrates on dialogue and how to say more with fewer words...

The 'snapshot' nature of screen drama

Every story ever told is a collection of fragments. We don't recount every scene or detail that happened along the way, we select what we choose to tell (and leave out) and structure it into a good tale – even when we tell a joke.

Screen storytelling – and the screenplay – is the most fragmentary form of storytelling there is (after comic books). A film's story may take place over several days (or, as in *Driving Miss Daisy*, several decades) but you only have two hours of screen time to tell it in. So you select those fragments which create something that maintains the illusion of being a coherent and cohesive whole story.

If a novel or stage play – with its capacity to digress, address the audience directly, examine psychological insights, etc. – may be equated to making a home video, then screen drama can be seen as a series of snapshot photographs (i.e. scenes) brought together to create a larger overall picture. It is your job to choose the right snapshots – and learn what to *omit* – and assemble them in the order that is the most dramatically effective, drawing out the maximum emotional impact.

How do you decide what to omit? You leave out anything that the audience can *deduce* for itself. If a woman in an office says she is hungry and is going out to get a sandwich, what are the possible scenes? Let's consider the obvious ones:

1 Office. Pam says she's hungry and is going to get a sandwich.

2 Office, near door. Pam puts on her coat and exits.

3 Stairs. Pam descends the stairs and reaches the street door. She exits.

4 Street. Pam emerges from the door and crosses the street to the sandwich bar.

5 Sandwich bar. Pam enters from the street and queues at the counter.

6 Queue. Pam moves slowly in the queue and finally reaches the counter.

7 Counter. Pam orders a sandwich, waits as it is being made, and is given it in a bag.

8 Shop. Pam takes the bag to a nearby table and sits down.

9 Table. Pam opens the bag, takes out the sandwich and lifts it to her mouth.

10 Mouth. Pam takes a huge bite out of the sandwich. Now she's happy.

Now *you* decide which are the most meaningful steps in the above story. Choose the smallest necessary ones to tell this story coherently. Leave out the steps you think the audience can deduce. To leave steps in, ask yourself: is this meaningful to the story? does this move the story forward? would it damage the sense of the story if it were left out?

Dialogue
Dialogue is verbal action which pushes the story forward and which is derived from the character's needs within the scene.

'Sometimes you steal dialogue you hear. But normally the way I write dialogue is: I have an idea of how long the dialogue should be – one page, two, three pages, how much the scene will support, and how many points I have to make in the dialogue – either information points or character development points. Then I just start working out conversation... using what seems natural to get from one point to another.'

Paul Schrader,
writer: *Taxi Driver,*
Raging Bull

Dialogue is the easiest way to impart story and character information. Hence, most new screenwriters will tend to over-emphasise dialogue above the other elements, but the sources of information in a screenplay should be shared by all the script's components.

Screenwriting is about learning how best and most appropriately to use *all* the means of expression: visual action (physical and decision), props, sounds, setting, context, subtext, etc. In general, dialogue should be the last resort of the screenwriter after all the other means of expression have been tried and found wanting.

Did you notice how spare the dialogue was in *Witness*? Did it work against your appreciation and understanding of the story and characters, or did it say more by saying less?

'Never let an actor talk unless he has something to say.'

John Huston,
director

Film is primarily a visual medium. Images, not words, are your basic currency. Hence the accepted rule is: *show, don't tell*. Despite the popularity of Quentin Tarantino's clever and entertaining 'plotless dialogue' (he's also a director, remember), it is still always preferable to show someone exhibiting a trait rather than telling it in dialogue. Even though TV is more dialogue driven than feature films, the TV writer should still conceive their script visually. Think visual: visualise your character, their behaviour details – body language, gestures, unconscious looks, habits, etc. – as you write your dialogue. And remember, characters interact.

Dialogue performs certain functions:

- providing information
- advancing the story onward and upward
- deepening the characters by revealing emotion, mood, feel, intent (via subtext) and by telling us what would be difficult, time-consuming or ponderous via character action
- revealing incidents and information (especially motivation) from the past, i.e. from the backstory, so that dialogue can avoid the need for flashbacks
- adding to the rhythm and pace of the script by the ambience it contributes to each scene and contributing to the style of the script (snappy and witty like *Butch Cassidy and The Sundance Kid*, *Maverick*; sparse like *Witness*, *Death in Venice*; distinctive like *Blade Runner*, *Brazil*, etc.)
- connecting scenes and shots by providing continuity
- suggesting the presence of objects, events or persons not seen by using off-screen (o.s.) dialogue.

Ideally, all the dialogue your characters speak should be caused by their need to get something in that scene or in a later scene. The true nature of good screen dialogue is that it comes from, is caused by and is driven by the immediate needs of your character at that specific point in the scene and that juncture of the plot, and also by their longer-term needs of the screenplay story.

Screen dialogue is not everyday conversation. What you strive for is *effective* dialogue, to give the *illusion* of real conversation. Effective dialogue sounds natural; it conveys the sense of real speech even though it is more structured than the wanderings of everyday speech. Effective dialogue has more economy and directness than real-life conversation.

Make a recording of people conversing, then listen to it; their dialogue is full of half-completed sentences, 'ers' and 'ums', hesitations and repetitions, rambling, overlapping and rarely focused – the *tone* is conversational, non-literary.

As in conversation, effective screen dialogue is essentially oblique, more naturalistic than, say, stage dialogue. Screenwriting uses all the hesitations, half-sentences, etc. of everyday speech, but the dialogue is condensed.

Screenwriting is typically lean and economic. Effective dialogue is sparsely written, with short sentences of simple construction, using simple, informal words. Speeches are brief and crisp. Screen dialogue is written for the ear, to be listened to, not for the eye to read. The basic principle of dialogue (as with all screenplay description) is:

Say More With Less

Dialogue *can* convey what a character thinks or tells us what is going on in their mind, but it can also be one of the dangers; it encourages novice writers to be lazy.

Screen dialogue words are used more for their implicit rather than explicit meaning. What is important in dialogue is not the literal meaning of the words used, but the meaning being conveyed in the circumstances of that scene. What is not said, or is left unsaid, can be as important as what is spoken.

Dialogue should fit the character, their mood and emotions in the particular situation, with a rhythm and individuality of expression typical of that character. Make your dialogue sound like the character, not the writer. One test is to take the dialogue in your scene and try swapping the speeches around and get those words spoken by your other character. If they can be switched with little evident distinction, then your characters and dialogue have probably not been effectively individualised.

Dialogue works best when it is underwritten and understated. Excessive emotion and spouting platitudes lead to melodrama. And when you *do* get an emotional dialogue scene, it must be in keeping with the character and their own personal speech patterns. Likewise, avoid clichés and stock phrases, unless they are part of the way that character always speaks.

Most screen dialogue exchanges are short and snappy, speeches bounce off each other like ping-pong, with one piece of dialogue hooking into or causing the next line, building up a momentum. Long single speeches stretching on and on for half a page or more will only alienate your audience. A reader, upon their initial flick-through fanning of your script, will notice any great slabs of dialogue. It turns them off; to them it indicates that the writer does not understand the accepted rules of writing screen dialogue. If you must have long speeches in your script, you had better have a good reason for them (for example Gordon Gekko's 'greed is good' speech in *Wall Street* is his whole philosophy of existence). So avoid long speeches; cut them out or into groups of smaller speeches. If you must, use very sparingly.

Be aware too of the role of silence: what is not said in a scene can be just as important as what is spoken. Actors and directors must learn to use silence as a tool in their box of effects – so should you. Remember, dialogue can be used off-screen (o.s.), or without sound (M.O.S.).

Some tips.

- Avoid 'passing-the-time-of-day' dialogue: greetings, polite nothings, goodbyes, etc.
- Don't repeat information in dialogue that has already occurred elsewhere in the dialogue; beginner's scripts are full of these repetitions.
- Avoid dialect and writing phonetically: tell the reader when you introduce the character they speak with a Scots/New Jersey/whatever accent. The occasional 'gonna' or 'ain't' is fine but don't overdo it. Script readers don't like reading phonetic dialogue – write it in readable English and let the actors do their jobs.
- If you want to create emphasis try to do it without using exclamation marks; never italicise dialogue; don't use capitals (except rarely); an occasional underlining is okay.
- Not every question asked in dialogue needs to be answered. The use of silence, a reaction, or non-reaction can be as/more powerful than dialogue (e.g. *Witness*). Not every question needs to be answered with the most obvious reply. An oblique open or indirect answer may reveal more about the state of mind of the responding character.

Extract 7.5: 'I Never Read Much', *Letters to Alice on First Reading Jane Austen* by Fay Weldon

Letters to Alice on First Reading Jane Austen is a book of letters to a fictional niece from her aunt. In these letters, the aunt tries to explain the value of literature and the process of writing. The aunt is a published novelist and the niece is trying to write her first book while still at college.

Somerset, March

My dear Alice,

How can I possibly tell you how to run your life? I am a novelist and your aunt, not a seer. I suppose I could offer a few general rules. For example:

1. Love your mother if you possibly can, since she is the source of your life.
2. Love men if you possibly can, since they are the source of your gratification.
3. Reform yourself, as well as the world.
4. Agree with your accusers, loudly and clearly. They will shut up sooner.
5. Worry less about what other people think of you, and more about what you think of them.

I shall leave 6, 7, 8, 9 and 10 blank, for you to fill in yourself. Revise them every New Year's Day. The real Secret of Life lies in Constant Rule Revision.

I can offer, more sensibly, a few general rules about writing:

(a) Show your work to no one, not to friend, nor spouse, nor anyone. They know no better than you, but will have to say something. The publisher or producer, eventually, will say yes or no, which are the only words you need to hear.

You won't observe this rule, so:

(b) What others say are your faults, your weaknesses, may if carried to extremes, be your virtues, your strengths. *I* don't like too many adjectives or adverbs – I say if a noun or a verb is worth describing, do it properly, take a sentence to do it. There's no hurry. Don't say 'the quick brown fox jumped over the lazy dog'. Say, 'it was at this moment that the fox jumped over the dog. The fox was brown as the hazelnuts in the tree hedgerows, and quick as the small stream that ran beside, and the dog too lazy to so much as turn his head.' Or something. Writing is more than just the making of a series of comprehensible statements: it is the gathering in of connotations; the harvesting of them, like blackberries in a good season, ripe and heavy, snatched from among the thorns of logic.

Having thus discouraged the apprentice writer from over-use of adjectives, I turn at once to Iris Murdoch and find she will use eighteen of them in a row. It works. What is weakness in small quantities, is style in overdose. So be wary of anyone who tries to teach you to write. Do it yourself. Stand alone. You will never be better than your own judgement, and you will never be satisfied with what you do. Ambition will, and should, always outstrip achievement.

(c), (d), (e) and (f) you can fill in for yourself.

You tell me the plot of your novel in a nutshell. It sounds perfectly dreadful. But then so does *Pride and Prejudice* in a nutshell. (I know! Witches used to go to sea in nutshells? Wrong again! Eggshells, a friend says. That's why children turn their eaten boiled eggs over and smash the shells. To thwart the witches. And I'd thought it was just their general tendency to leave me to clear up the detail of their self-expression. But I broke my eggshells as a child: so did your mother: I expect you do too. It is the kind of thing that gets handed on like life expectancy, rolling acres and cold sores.)

I will tell you that the main fault of young writers is their habit of writing about the love lives of themselves and their friends, since this is so boring to the truly adult reader – inasmuch as what strikes the young as exciting and amazing is to the more experienced observer trite beyond belief, and boring too, and I will suggest that you wait until you have met an actual trouble or two, and know yourself a little better, and lose your good opinion of yourself, and get on with your studies, as your mother and father are so anxious that you should and then events will prove me wrong and you right. It is the kind of thing that happens.

I am wrong about things two times out of five. My general impression about other people is that they are wrong two-and-a-half times out of five. Can this be success? I know a brain surgeon. She plunges about with lasers in the brains of people who will die if she does nothing. Sometimes she cures them totally, sometimes she kills them quickly, sometimes she reduces them to long-lasting vegetables. But someone has to do something. And her vegetation rate, as it's called, is two out of ten and not three out of ten, as it is with her colleagues, and her death rate the same, so she is considered The Best. And is. And people queue up – if people in comas can be said to queue up – for her services.

Your novel is about a young girl studying English Literature who falls in love with her professor, who is married to someone unlovable, and how her boyfriend reacts, which is not as expected. (It's how *I* expect, who have some knowledge of human depravity.) He has an affair with Unlovable. It is all, obviously, autobiographical. My advice to you is, consider the nature of Unlovable. You may be wrong about her.

May I also suggest that your falling in love is an example of those diversionary tactics which afflict the writer – (I have already described them) – because in your earlier account of this novel it concerned a young girl studying English Literature who falls in love with a fellow student (male) and so escapes incipient lesbianism. By changing your allegiance to the professor you have altered the course of your novel – or should, unless you want it to be merely episodic – and delayed its finishing.

Why not fall out of love with the professor and go back to your first draft? But I'm afraid you won't. I'm afraid you'll then need a third draft about a young girl falling *out* of love with a married professor – and so on and so on. And will boyfriend then come back to you? He may not, you see. *You* know he's part of your fiction, but he, rightly or wrongly, believes he's living in a real world.

There's no end to it if you go on like this, nor, I fear, of the novel. Novels are not meant to be diaries, you know.

Your loving Aunt

Extract 7.6: *Tips for Journalists*, The Poynter Institute

This advice is taken from the website of The Poynter Institute in the USA, a school for journalists, future journalists and teachers of journalism. It includes a range of suggestions for developing as a newswriter.

If I Were a Carpenter: The Tools of a Writer by Roy Peter Clark

It is helpful at times to think that writing is like carpentry, where you work from a plan and use the tools you've stored on your workbench. You can borrow a writing tool whenever you like. And here's the secret: You don't have to return it. You can pass it on to another writer without losing it.

Below, Poynter's Roy Peter Clark shares some of the writing tools he has borrowed from reporters and editors, authors of books on writing, and from teachers and coaches.

Sentences and paragraphs

1 Begin sentences with subjects and verbs, letting subordinate elements branch off to the right. Even a very long sentence can be clear and powerful when subject and verb make meaning early.
2 Use verbs in their strongest form, the simple present or past tense. Strong verbs create action, save words, and reveal the players. Beware of adverbs. Too often, they dilute the meaning of the verb or repeat it: 'The building was completely destroyed.'
3 Place strong words at the beginning of sentences and paragraphs, and at the end. The period acts as a stop sign. Any word next to the period plays jazz.

Language

4 Observe word territory. Do not repeat a key word without a given space, unless you intend a specific effect.

5 Play with words, even in serious stories.

6 Dig for the concrete and specific: the name of the dog and the brand of the beer. Details help readers see the story.

7 When tempted by clichés, seek original images. Make word lists, free-associate, be surprised by language.

8 Prefer the simple over the technical: shorter words and paragraphs at the points of greatest complexity.

9 Strive for the mythic, symbolic and poetic. Recognise that common themes of newswriting (homecoming, conquering obstacles, loss and restoration) have deep roots in the culture of storytelling.

Effects

10 For clarity, slow the pace of information. Short sentences make the reader move slowly. Time to think. Time to learn. See what I mean?

11 Control the pace of the story by varying sentence length. Long sentences create a glow that carries readers down a stream of understanding, creating an effect that Don Fry calls 'steady advance'. Or stop a reader short.

12 Show and tell. Begin at the bottom of the ladder of abstraction, at the level of bloody knives and rosary beads, of wedding rings and baseball cards. Then ascend to the top to summarise and analyse, discovering meaning in the world's random details.

13 Reveal telling character traits and the glories of human speech. Avoid adjectives when describing people. Don't say 'enthusiastic' or 'talkative', but

create a scene in which the person reveals those characteristics to the reader.

14 Strive for 'voice', the illusion that the writer is speaking directly to the reader. Read the story aloud to hear if it sounds like you.

Structure

15 Take advantage of narrative opportunities. You want to write stories, not articles. Think of action, conflict, motivation, setting, chronology and dialogue.

16 Place gold coins along the path. Don't load all your best stuff high in the story. Space special effects throughout the story, encouraging readers to find them and be delighted by them.

17 Use sub-headlines to index the story for the readers. This tool tests the writer's ability to find, and label, the big parts of the story.

18 Repeat key words or images to 'chain' the story together. Repetition works only if you intend it.

19 In storytelling, three is the magic number. Four is too many. Two is not enough.

20 Write endings to create closure.

Roy Peter Clark is The Poynter Institute's senior scholar and a member of the Reporting, Writing and Editing faculty.

Guide to Writing Headlines by John Russial

Writing Leads

The lead, or the beginning of a story, is an important writing element. Some writers believe that if you don't capture the reader in the beginning, the reader will not want to continue reading the piece. The lead entices, entertains and informs the reader. A lead can be a sentence or many sentences.

You can experiment with several leads. Take the suggestions from other writers below:

Dialogue
A character in the writing speaks.
Example: 'Where's papa going with that axe?' said Fern to her mother as they were setting the table for breakfast. (*Charlotte's Web* by E. B. White, taken from *What a Writer Needs* by Ralph Fletcher)

Introducing the narrator
Sometimes the writer designs the lead to introduce the character who will, in turn, tell the story.
Example: I live at 165 East 95 Street, New York City, and I'm going to stay here forever. My mother and father are moving out West.
(Taken from *What a Writer Needs* by Ralph Fletcher)

Ask a question
Example: I am also a city boy, a city boy who likes his comforts, a city boy who, despite himself, is nervous about being completely alone in the wilderness of Florida. What if the raw oysters I ate for lunch give me hepatitis? Or, more likely, what if I fall off my bike and bust a collarbone?
(Taken from *Free to Write* by Roy Peter Clark)

Use a series of paraphrases for effect
Example: A 42-year-old man. A man of heart and soul.
(Taken from *What a Writer Needs* by Ralph Fletcher)

Newsy
Answers the 5 W's. (WHO WHAT WHERE WHY WHEN)
Example: 'An Air Florida Jetliner taking off from National Airport in a snowstorm crashed into a crowded bridge this afternoon and broke as it plunged into the Potomac River, leaving at least 10 persons dead and more than 40 missing, according to unofficial police estimates.'
(Taken from *Free to Write* by Roy Peter Clark)

Personification

A nonhuman functions as a human.

Example: Fall does not march into Florida like a brass band. That happens in New England or North Carolina, where blazing leaves are a tourist attraction. In our state, fall more or less slips through the back door a month after many people have all but given up on its arrival. Fall comes whistling softly.

(Taken from *Real Florida* by Jeff Klinkenberg)

Appeals to senses

Example: Tommie Smith put pine saplings under the black kettle to keep the fire going. She dumpled pork fat into the kettle, and as it melted she added water and lye and stirred with a wood spoon. The mixture was neither too thick nor too liquid. She could tell it was going to be a good batch.

The smoke curled into the oaks and pines above and into Tommie's face. She blinked and stepped back. Then the wind shifted and she attacked the kettle again with her spoon. Her large arms showed muscle as she stirred hard. She wanted everything to be just right for the people who had come to north Florida's Stephen Foster State Folk Culture Centre here to watch her make her specialty – lye soap.

(Taken from *Real Florida* by Jeff Klinkenberg)

Interesting fact

Example: The first thing you notice is the cats, cats said to be descended from the pets he kept so long ago. They are on his stone wall and in his banyan trees, on his front porch and on his veranda above, weird six-toed cats everywhere. You walk through his gate, stepping over a cat, as a matter of fact, and hand over your admission at 10:30 on one of those warm Key West mornings for which tourists pay plenty.

(Taken from *Real Florida* by Jeff Klinkenberg)

Describes surroundings

Example: Dark comes early to Withlacoochee State Forest. The sun dips behind the pines and the shadows lengthen and the night creatures reveal themselves. Armadillos crash through the palmettos. Bats flit over the dirt road where wildlife biologists Lenela Glass-Godwin and her husband, Jim, have parked their pickup. The Godwins are creatures of the night, too. They have come to listen to the opera.

(Taken from *Real Florida* by Jeff Klinkenberg)

Surprise humour

Example: Nicki Tomarelli was driving through Queens, New York. She had just eaten a big spicy lunch at an Indian restaurant, and suddenly found herself in desperate need of a bathroom. There! A Mobil gas station! She double-parked and raced inside – both bathrooms were locked. OUT OF ORDER. Nicki looked imploringly at one of the mechanics.

(Taken from *What a Writer Needs* by Ralph Fletcher)

This tip was adapted from a handout taken from Poynter's Janie Guilbault Fellowship programme to benefit Pinellas County public and private school reading and language arts teachers, as well as elementary and middle school students with an interest or talent in writing.

Clearer, Stronger Writing by Al Tompkins

1 Tell the story in three words of OTPS, one theme per story, one thought per sentence. Select, don't compress, what goes in your stories. The stuff that does not make it into the story will make great tags, follow ups, or additional material for Internet sites.

2 Tell complex stories through strong characters. Readers and viewers will remember what they feel longer than what they know. Characters help me

understand how the complex facts you uncovered affect people.

3 Objective copy, subjective sound. Let the characters evoke emotions, express feelings and give opinions in their soundbites. The journalists' copy should contain objective words, facts and truths.

4 Use active verbs, not passive ones. Consider the difference between 'the gun was found' and 'the boy found the gun'. Ask 'Who did what?' and you will write stronger and more informed stories.

5 No subjective adjectives. Your lawyer and your viewers will thank you. No more 'fantastic-unbelievable-gut wrenching' or 'mother's worst nightmare'.

6 Give viewers a sense for the passage of time in your story. Make me feel you have spent some time by showing me the character in more than one setting, in more than one situation.

7 Remember, leads tell me 'so what', stories tell me 'what' and tags tell me 'what's next'.

Al Tompkins is the Broadcast/Online Group Leader at The Poynter Institute. 'Clearer, Stronger Writing', was published originally in *The Effective Editor* by Foster Davis and Karen F. Dunlap.

Activities

The extracts in this section have reflected or given advice on the writing process. The following questions suggest ways in which you might use this section.

1   As an exercise, undertake the activities suggested by the writers – for example, you might find the practice of imitating sentence structure in 'On Imitation' an interesting process that will help your own writing and also aid your understanding of another author's skill and technique.

2   Use the advice to redraft a piece you have already written – for example, check your use of adverbs and adjectives as suggested by Fay Weldon in 'I Never Read Much', or the structure of a literary essay using the model described in 'The English Exam' (page 192).

3   Try following the more extended guidelines to prepare a new piece of writing. You may also find it helpful to develop the skills you have already practised.

4   Use the guides/advice as a tool for analysing a piece of writing from this anthology or a set text/class reader – for example, how far does the extract from *Buffy the Vampire Slayer* comply with the advice given in *Screenwriting*?

'The English Exam'

1   This piece is written as a response to a GCSE English Language exam question requiring descriptive writing – the student has based his writing on his experience of the English Literature exam he has already taken. In this piece, he has managed to both fulfil the criteria for a very successful piece of descriptive writing, and also to reflect on the process of writing about literature for an exam.

    a What features make this a successful piece of writing?

    b What does he identify as the important elements of answering a literature question?

    c What do you feel he is saying about the experience of writing under conditions of pressure?

    d How does he manage to keep the reader entertained?

2 What useful points might you glean from this piece about:

    a Answering a literature question well?

    b Writing a good descriptive piece?

Very Short Stories

Edited by Mike Royston

This book contains a collection of very short stories from a range of genres chosen to interest and appeal to students at Key Stage 3. Some of the stories are by well-known authors such as Paul Jennings, Jan Mark, Susan Price and Ray Bradbury. Others are by new authors. Each of them can be read in less than ten minutes and offers an example of a well-structured and complete text.

The activities at the end of the book are based on identified sentence and text level objectives of the *Framework for Teaching English*. Speaking and listening objectives are also covered.

These stories have been chosen to enable students to read for meaning, understand the author's craft and apply what they have learnt to their own writing. They are also accessible stories that will arrest the attention and engage the imagination of all students across Key Stage 3.

Age 11+ ISBN 0 435 13058 7

Acknowledgements

The publishers gratefully acknowledge the following for permission to reproduce copyright material. Every effort has been made to trace copyright holders, but in some cases has proved impossible. The publishers would be happy to hear from any copyright holder that has not been acknowledged.

Extract from *Teach Yourself Screenwriting* by Raymond G. Frensham, published by Hodder Educational; Bloomsbury for an extract from *The Princess Bride* by William Goldman, published by Bloomsbury; The Random House Group Limited for an extract from *Have The Men Had Enough* by Margaret Forster, published by Chatto & Windus; University of Oregon for an extract from 'Gender Speech Issues' by Cyndi Pattee, found at http://logos.uoregon.edu/explore/socioling/gender2.html; NAACP c/o Gordon Feinblatt LLC, USA for 'A Telephone Call' and 'Unfortunate Coincidence' by Dorothy Parker, from *The Penguin*, published by Penguin Books and Gerald Duckworth; A. P. Watt Limited for an extract from *The Sheep-Pig* by Dick King-Smith; Curtis Brown Group Limited London on behalf of Mil Millington for an extract from http://homepage.ntlworld.com/ mil.millington/things.html. Copyright © Mil Millington 2002; 'I Love You It's True' by Carole Stewart from 'Watchers and Seekers' published by The Women's Press; David Higham Associates Limited for an extract from *Horses Make a Landscape Look More Beautiful* by Alice Walker, published by The Women's Press; Twentieth Century Fox for an extract from 'Buffy The Vampire Slayer' © 1999 Twentieth Century Fox Television. All rights reserved; Lonely Planet Publications for an extract from http://lonelyplanet.com/ destinations/antarctica/antarctica/culture.htm © Copyright 2002 Lonely Planet Publications. All rights reserved. www.lonelyplanet.com; International Association of Antarctica Tour Operators, USA for an extract from www.iaato.org/visitor_guide.html; Atlas Travel for an extract from www.atlastravelweb.com; Mirror Syndications for an extract from The Mirror, Wednesday May 21st 1913; Scott Ferris Associates for an extract from *Scott and Amundsen* by Roland Huntford, published by Hodder 1979. © Roland Huntford 1979, 1983; The Random House Group Limited for an extract from *Terra Incognita* by Sara Wheeler, published by Jonathan Cape; The Observer for 'In from the cold...' by Robert McFarlane from The Observer, 7th October 2001. © Robert McFarlane 2001; David Higham Associates Limited for an extract from *Bernice Bobs Her Hair* by F Scott Fitzgerald, published by Replica; The Observer for 'It's a boy thing' by Lyn Gardiner, from The Observer, 9th October 2001. © Lyn Gardiner 2001; Bill Greenwell for 'The Pig on Ted Hughes' by Bill Greenwell; Campbell Thomson & McLaughlin Limited for 'Jane Austen 1775–1817 – Pride and Porringers' by E. O. Parrott from *Imitations of Immortality*, edited by E. O. Parrott and published by Penguin Books. © E. O. Parrott 1986; Adbusters for an extract from www.adbusters.org; Bonnie Bierthaler for posters from www.badvertising.org © 1986 Bonnie Bierthaler, BADvertising Institute, Xiamen, Fujian, China. Phone: 86 592 218 2565, Fax: 86 592 218 0841, email bv@badvertising.org, order posters or slide kits c/o NJ GASP..., regina@njgasp.org; Faber and Faber Limited for an extract from 'Kit Bag List' from *Moon Country* by Simon Armitage and Glyn Maxwell, published by Faber and Faber; Penguin Books UK for an extract from *High Fidelity* by Nick Hornby, published by Penguin Books 2000. Copyright © Nick Hornby 1996; 'Deeper than Colour' by Ijeoma Inyama; Macmillan UK for an extract from *On Becoming A Writer* by Dorothea Brande, published by Macmillan UK; Joe Swarbrick for 'The English Exam' by Joe Swarbrick; Faber and Faber Limited for an extract from *Poetry in the Making* by Ted Hughes, published by Faber and Faber; Fay Weldon and her agent Sheil Land Associates Limited, London for an extract from *Letters to Alice* by Fay Weldon. © Copyright Fay Weldon; The Poynter Institute for extracts from www.poynter.org.

Founding Editors: Anne and Ian Serraillier

Chinua Achebe Things Fall Apart
David Almond Skellig
Maya Angelou I Know Why the Caged Bird Sings
Margaret Atwood The Handmaid's Tale
Jane Austen Pride and Prejudice
Stan Barstow Joby: A Kind of Loving
Nina Bawden Carrie's War; The Finding; Humbug
Malorie Blackman Tell Me No Lies; Words Last Forever
Charlotte Brontë Jane Eyre
Emily Brontë Wuthering Heights
Melvin Burgess and Lee Hall Billy Elliot
Betsy Byars The Midnight Fox; The Pinballs; The Eighteenth Emergency
Victor Canning The Runaways
Sir Arthur Conan Doyle Sherlock Holmes Short Stories
Susan Cooper King of Shadows
Robert Cormier Heroes
Roald Dahl Danny; The Champion of the World; The Wonderful
Story of Henry Sugar; George's Marvellous Medicine; The Witches;
Boy; Going Solo; Matilda; My Year
Anita Desai The Village by the Sea
Charles Dickens A Christmas Carol; Great Expectations; A Charles
Dickens Selection
Berlie Doherty Granny was a Buffer Girl; Street Child
Roddy Doyle Paddy Clarke Ha Ha Ha
George Eliot Silas Marner
Anne Fine The Granny Project
Leon Garfield Six Shakespeare Stories
Ann Halam Dr Franklin's Island
Thomas Hardy The Withered Arm and Other Wessex Tales; The Mayor
of Casterbridge
Ernest Hemmingway The Old Man and the Sea; A Farewell to Arms
Barry Hines A Kestrel For A Knave
Nigel Hinton Buddy; Buddy's Song
Anne Holm I Am David

How many have you read?